What We Mean by the American Dream

Stories We Tell about
Meritocracy

Doron Taussig

ILR Press
an imprint of Cornell University Press
Ithaca and London

First published 2021 by Cornell University Press

Printed in the United States of America

Library of Congress Cataloging-in-Publication Data

Names: Taussig, Doron, author.
Title: What we mean by the American dream : stories we tell about meritocracy / Doron Taussig.
Description: Ithaca [New York] : ILR press, an imprint of Cornell University Press, 2021. | Includes bibliographical references and index.
Identifiers: LCCN 2020027292 (print) | LCCN 2020027293 (ebook) | ISBN 9781501754685 (hardcover) | ISBN 9781501754708 (pdf) | ISBN 9781501754692 (epub)
Subjects: LCSH: Social mobility—United States—Psychological aspects. | American Dream. | Success—United States—Psychological aspects. | United States—Economic conditions—21st century. | United States—Social conditions—21st century.
Classification: LCC HN90.S65 T37 2021 (print) | LCC HN90.S65 (ebook) | DDC 306.0973—dc23
LC record available at https://lccn.loc.gov/2020027292
LC ebook record available at https://lccn.loc.gov/2020027293

Once I understood what was making America such a dangerous, unhappy nation of people who had nothing to do with real life, I resolved to shun storytelling. I would write about life. Every person would be exactly as important as any other. All facts would also be given equal weightiness. Nothing would be left out. Let others bring order to chaos. I would bring chaos to order, instead.

—Kurt Vonnegut, *Breakfast of Champions*

Contents

What We Mean by the
American Dream

Introduction

Eric and Philip Mitchell grew up in the same home, at the same time, but have had very different experiences of twenty-first-century America. The Mitchell boys were raised, both agree, in a lower-income, mostly black neighborhood in Philadelphia. Their father worked a white-collar job, and their mother was a nurse and then a homemaker. Both feel blessed but not spoiled by their parents' support: Eric says it was a financial struggle after their mother stopped working, and Philip talks about not forgetting where he comes from. When they were kids, Philip recalls, their father used to drive them past housing projects, ask if they wanted to live there, and tell them to get scholarships to college. Both attended special admissions public high schools. Both got scholarships to college.

Eric, who is twenty-eight, studied computer science, landed a tech job with a large company, then got laid off because of budget cuts. He applied for a job as a deliveryman. "What are you doing here?" the boss asked as he looked over Eric's résumé. "If I were you I'd get up and walk right out right now." Eric got the job, but before long his manager from his tech job called and invited him to come back. He landed a new position, established himself, and negotiated a raise. He has plans to start his own business and generally feels well positioned for the future.

"It's not luck," Eric says, sitting in a downtown coffee shop. "Things do seem to just fall in place for me." What he means is that God smiles on him: "It has nothing to do with me, it really doesn't," he says. Pushed to elaborate, though, he says that God gave him his opportunities and talents, but "the reason why [I got hired and promoted] is because of how good I am at what I do." He hustles, he says, and thinks his confident demeanor helps to separate him from the pack. His confidence is indeed striking. When I ask Eric about other directions his life could have taken, one of the possibilities he mentions is that he might have been an NBA player had he not refused to wear corrective goggles when he played ball as a kid. It's an optimistic scenario. Eric appears to be of about average height. In 2020, there were two active NBA players listed at five foot nine or shorter.

One of the charged questions many of us grapple with as Americans is whether we have earned what we have and advanced to where we deserve to be in society. Eric—with some hesitation—says he has. "I may not have had to work as hard to get certain opportunities that other people have," he says, "but I have had to work hard once I got them, so I think I have earned it." Nor does he think he is simply a product of circumstance. "I don't think that people born into my same circumstances would have the same success," he says. Take his brother, for example. "Not to put my little brother on blast or anything like that," he tells me, but "my brother doesn't have the drive that I do in certain instances."

Philip, twenty-five, apologizes for being late to meet me after Eric put us in touch. All the warning lights came on in his car, and his mechanic said just looking at it would cost $125, which Philip didn't have. A bigger concern than meeting up with some interviewer was getting to his job stocking shelves at a big-box store, a job Philip needs but decidedly does not want. He has a degree in communications and expertise in audio editing, and he wishes to use them. Like his brother, Philip lost his first gig out of college when the training program he was in was terminated due to budget cuts. A position Eric then helped him land was eliminated due to cuts too. He tried to work as a mailman but failed the driving test, which happened to take place during a snowstorm. By the time we met he felt "pretty bummed out"; he was qualified but not getting calls back.

Philip offers a very different explanation for his problems from the one his brother gave. "I paid my dues," he says. "I do really good work." But even in the rare instances when he's gotten opportunities, they have evaporated "through no fault of my own"—such as when the training program he was in got shut down. "Every time my foot's in the door, they close the door and lock it." He thinks he's earned better than he's gotten from his communications career thus far. He should at least be out of his parents' house by now, he says.

"[I did] what everyone says, how the American Dream works. . . . I came in, I worked hard, did what I was supposed to, I listened, I got my grades, I got the degree, I got the scholarships, got the experience, I got what [people] said needs to be gotten, and I haven't gotten a damn thing." The problem, he thinks, is bigger than him. "It's more of an America thing. . . . It's happening to everybody." He thinks there might be a generational problem in this country, whereby people who worked hard to achieve success now make sure their kids don't have to go through the same struggle. "But for the ones that still have to work hard, it's like we have to work two or three times as hard."

It is not shocking to hear a person who feels successful say he's earned his success, nor to hear a person frustrated with his career blame larger forces. But there are a couple of wrinkles worth observing in Eric's and Philip's explanations. For one thing, Eric expresses skepticism similar to his brother's about the state of the American economy. "That whole American Dream of, if you put the work in, it'll pay off in the end, I feel like it's been tainted a bit, because there are a lot of people that are putting in a lot of work, and they're not getting their just due, and I feel like there are a lot of people that aren't putting in as much work, but because they have certain connections, they get more."

This observation seemed to me potentially at odds with Eric's explanation of his success. Why is his *own* pursuit of the American Dream going so well? He explains that there are ways some people make it work. "You gotta know where to push," he says. "You gotta work hard, but you gotta know who to talk to." He believes the reason he knows where to push has to do with his father's lessons and example. Of course, Philip had the same father. But Eric suspects his brother was pampered. "I feel like things have been handed a little more to my brother from my parents, and I think that made him a little soft as far as, now he thinks things should be handed to him." As an example, Eric observes that growing up, Philip had a computer, whereas Eric had to go to a friend's house to use one. Eric is not sure that Philip knows where and how to push.

The second wrinkle is that Philip remains hopeful about his prospects. "I do think things are going to work out," he says. This too sparked my curiosity: Why would Philip expect to succeed in a system that he says, with great conviction, isn't working for people like him? "The way I see it is, you can't keep beating and beating and beating and nothing happens—something has to give."

The Myth of the Myth of Meritocracy

Americans are supposed to believe that we live in a meritocracy. It's part of our national mythology and a key tenet of the

American Dream: this is the land of opportunity, anyone can grow up to be president, and most of us end up in our working lives about where we deserve to be on the basis of effort and ability. Our belief in this mythology is supposed to help explain why we accept our position in an unequal society and take responsibility for our own lot in life. But when we look at the ways Americans describe individual success and failure, we see something a bit different.

This book is about how Americans account for the role of merit in our lives—not the reality of American meritocracy but the perception of it. I spoke with Eric, Philip, and a diverse group of fifty-eight other Americans, and examined stories told in national media about thirty prominent figures from politics, business, and sports, as part of an effort to understand our thoughts on the matter. I asked how we explain why people end up where we do in our working lives, how we understand the relationship between an individual and his or her circumstances, how we grapple with perceived advantages and disadvantages, and what standards we use to assess whether an individual has earned or deserves a job, an opportunity, a termination, a paycheck, a fortune. I also asked how we square our thoughts on individual lives with our perceptions of the American social system. In the chapters that follow, we hear from an ex-con struggling to get on his feet who believes he's earned his predicament ("and it's crippling"); the daughter of a wealthy doctor studying to be a therapist ("My dad has a lot of money. . . . I might not be where I am if I didn't have that kind of security"); a CEO who calls himself "the definition of meritocracy" (and supported Bernie Sanders in 2016); and the owner of a heating and air-conditioning company who worked his way up cleaning oil burners ("My whole life, all I needed was a job"). We also hear about how American media explain and debate the successes and failures of public figures such as Sheryl Sandberg ("Hard work and results *should* be recognized by others, but when they aren't, advocating for oneself becomes necessary"[1]), Stephen Curry, and Hillary Clinton ("She has been successful in life when she has made herself a victim"[2]).

These conversations have become especially pointed in recent years. Between ballooning inequality, a string of high-profile failures by ruling elites (both the Iraq War and the collapse of the global economy in 2008 were overseen by people who "rose to the top" of American society), and more opportunities via the Internet and social media for public expressions of dissent, the early twenty-first century has provided ample evidence for and access to concern about the American Dream. Eric and Philip are hardly alone: the proportion of Americans who believe our economic system is "basically fair" dropped from 68 percent in 1998 to 50 percent in 2013, according to Gallup polling, and a Pew Research Center survey conducted in 2019 found that seven in ten American adults believe our economic system unfairly favors the powerful.[3] The 2012 presidential election seemed in large part a debate over whether American meritocracy was fact or fantasy, with Barack Obama's admonition to business owners that "you didn't build that"[4] pitted against Mitt Romney's description of 47 percent of Americans as people "who are dependent upon government, who believe that they are victims."[5] By the 2016 election, Americans' concern about whether our system rewards merit appeared to transcend political boundaries, and the relevant question seemed not fact versus fantasy but farce. The eventual winner rose to political prominence calling the nation's economy and political system "rigged," then took office and put his son-in-law in charge of everything.

As I write this in 2020, the country has been shut down to prevent the spread of COVID-19, and the implications for the way we think about what is earned and deserved have the potential to be profound. People have lost jobs, money, and homes because of circumstances *obviously* outside their own control. Simultaneously, the Black Lives Matter movement has put racial inequality top of mind for many more Americans. I researched and wrote most of this book before any of this happened (the word "pandemic" did not appear in the first draft), but it's hard to imagine that by the time you read this, Americans will have settled into the confident belief that the country works. So this is a good time to ask how Americans think about what is earned and deserved.

The question of what is earned has long been found just beneath the surface of everyday stories, conversations, and social dynamics. It fuels the Brooklynite's shame about her parents helping to pay her rent, the baby boomer's pride about building his own business, the widespread resentment of the welfare recipient. It underpins debates about school admissions, hiring practices, and award shows. And it will almost certainly be an important component of forthcoming struggles over health care costs, relief efforts, and economic restructuring. Yet people are not often asked directly how they got where they are and what merit had to do with it. So I tried to put the question to some of us head-on.

What I found is that many of us *don't* actually view our lives through the lens of societal meritocracy, but neither do we need to think we live in a meritocracy to conclude that we, personally, have gotten or will get where we deserve. What Americans do, faced with the question of how we got where we are and whether we earned it, is to ask whether we have *done enough on our own* to warrant our position, using a set of fuzzy and subjective standards and stories to make the assessment. Our understanding of how life works and what it means to deserve something is more flexible and fluid than meritocratic mythology.

This distinction has important implications. Many Americans don't actually treat strict meritocracy as a condition for individual deservedness, because we are adept at using our storytelling skills to navigate potential contradictions between individual lives and the ideal. Our actual, less-than-meritocratic worldview can seem hypocritical and self-serving, particularly when people who have enjoyed big advantages proclaim that they've earned their success. Think of Donald Trump suggesting that *he* is the reason he became a real estate magnate, because (he says) he built so much on what his father gave him. A flexible approach to assessing what someone has earned makes it easier to start at a conclusion, whether based on desired self-image, identity, or politics, and work backward to justify it. It also makes it easier to dismiss or minimize unequal opportunities.

But I'm going to argue that our lukewarm relationship with meritocracy holds some promise as well. Critics of inequality often fall into a rhetorical trap wherein the solution to every shortcoming of meritocracy is more and better meritocracy. We call for better public schools, better admissions policies, etc. so that rewards can go to the truly deserving. But if Americans already understand that life is messy and society is unfair, we might do better to challenge the *ideal* of meritocracy rather than its execution. When public figures tell their stories, when journalists chronicle successes and failures, when teachers explain social dynamics, and when you and I consider and discuss our own lives, we could ask not just whether someone earned what he or she has but whether such a thing is possible. We could place less emphasis on who deserves resources and dignity—and then push for policies that do the same.

I won't argue for abandoning meritocratic principles altogether, which I think is neither realistic nor practical. Rather, I suggest some approaches to thinking and talking about individual success and failure that acknowledge meritocracy's inevitable shortcomings and evaluate people accordingly: approaches like highlighting random luck, admitting the role of unearned talent, celebrating success (and explaining failure) as a group endeavor, and criticizing undeserving elites without suggesting that a more deserving elite necessarily lies in wait to replace them. In short, inviting some skepticism about whether people really can earn it.

All of this, I recognize, is a long walk from where we are now. Americans have subscribed to the individual meritocratic ideal for a very long time.

Shark Tank Nation

Americans didn't come up with the idea of organizing a society around merit. Plato beat us to the punch when he called for a group of gifted "guardians," drawn from all classes, to be selected at age ten and raised to be rulers. But to live in American culture, from the SATs to welfare-to-work, from Horatio Alger to *Shark Tank*, is to swim in meritocratic waters.

The United States was conceived as a rejection of tyranny, and our founders, in search of some other form of social organization, decided that power belonged in the hands of the (white, male, landowning) people, all of whom they declared to be equal. But there was a tension here, beyond the obvious contradictions of slavery and patriarchy: even if all white male landowners were equal, only some of them were going to rule. And so while the founders posited that all men were equal in the eyes of God and the state, they also thought men should be sorted according to virtues, abilities, and talents. (Jefferson famously declared his belief in a "natural aristocracy of talents.") As if to make the point perfectly clear, the founders dubbed themselves the "Men of Merit."[6]

The idea of *equal opportunity* as a prerequisite for a merit-based society did not arise immediately; the opportunity of a vast frontier and the absence of a feudal system was enough to establish and send down through generations the premise that in the United States, men could rise according to their merits. This premise, of course, invites questions, not the least of which is what merit *is*, exactly.

Used as a verb, the word "merit" basically means "deserve."[7] One could say that a billionaire "merits" his success, but one could also say that a problem "merits" attention or even that a criminal "merits" a jail sentence. The verb is value-neutral. One would not say, however, that a criminal *has merit*—at least not in the context of a serious crime. As a noun, "merit" refers to positive characteristics, but it also still retains a hint of the notion of *deserving*: to have merit is to be good in a particular way that makes you deserve reward or recognition.

Now, most people don't go around talking explicitly about the role of "merit" in their lives, and plenty are unfamiliar with the term "meritocracy." So in my interviews and throughout this book, I use both the terms "earn" and "deserve" to describe the idea of achieving something due to merit. Neither verb is perfectly suited to the task. Earning a reward requires specific necessary actions, and some people would say, for example, that spots in a gifted kindergarten class could be distributed by merit without the kids' "earning" them per se. Meanwhile, not everything a person *deserves* is due to merit. You can deserve a chance, due process, medical care, etc. regardless of who you are or what you've done. But I would argue that, given appropriate context, both can convey the spirit of the American idea of positive characteristics justifying reward.

Even in this more colloquial usage, you can see the challenge for a society that wishes to organize itself around merit. The notion is, as Amartya Sen writes, "essentially underdefined."[8] Which characteristics are positive? What rewards do they justify? Merit is an empty vessel of a concept, and its meaning depends on how a particular society fills it in.

Consequently, Americans have made a habit of arguing about whether people in this country get what they deserve, and how to build a society in which they do. We began with a vague sense that successful people had merit because they were successful. The evident unfairness of the Gilded Age fueled dissatisfaction with this poorly articulated, tautological premise, and gradually American institutions such as the armed forces, the civil service, and universities began to attempt to measure and select for merit. In the early part of the twentieth century, most institutions came to focus on measuring intelligence, which was believed to be "a biologically based, unitary, quantifiable entity" and a "true" distinction between individuals.[9]

During this time the notion of equal opportunity and social support for the promotion of merit took hold. To this day people have many different convictions about what this should mean in practice: The absence of direct discrimination and nepotism? A comparable quality of primary education for all citizens? Free college for all?[10] But we began to grapple more with the idea of a functioning system as a prerequisite for meritorious achievement.

The actual term "meritocracy" was coined in England and popularized in 1958 by the British sociologist Michael Young as a *derogatory* description of a dystopian future in which all social positions are determined through intelligence testing. In Young's vision, people become perverse and cruel as a result: wealthy parents try to adopt high-IQ working-class children, superiors are dismissive of their objectively inferior subordinates, etc.[11] Here in America, however, the term was embraced as a description of what the country had always claimed to aspire to, and particularly of the social system that would promote a new group of elites to replace the WASP ruling class.[12] From today's vantage point, it is remarkable not only that the term "meritocracy" was used as a pejorative, but also that anyone's concern about meritocracy was that the testers would get it *right* and society would accept their verdicts. This is not what we generally worry about today.

Today, argue Stephen McNamee and Robert Miller, Americans conceive of merit as some combination of innate talents and abilities, attitude, hard work, and moral character, and we generally accept the premise that society should reward these qualities.[13] Our institutions profess to make decisions meritocratically; cultural totems like the NFL and *American Idol* tell meritocratic stories. We hold aloft the idea of "a social system as a whole in which individuals get ahead and earn rewards in direct proportion to their individual efforts and abilities."[14] We have come to see such a system as both efficient (because it puts the most qualified people in the right positions and incentivizes effort) and fundamentally fair (because it promises that people will get rewards in proportion to their contributions).[15] Only recently have we begun to grapple with arguments like Young's—that a functioning meritocracy would not in fact be efficient or fair. What we worry about instead is how well we are executing such a system. In debates over policies such as affirmative action, school choice, tax rates, etc., most participants present themselves as the promoters of true meritocracy.

How do we think we're doing? Back in 1973, two sociologists named Joan Huber and William Form articulated what they called the "dominant ideology" of the United States: that Americans generally believe we enjoy equal chances of success in our society; that success consequently is a result of effort, ability, and other individual qualities; and that to whatever extent we fall short of this ideal, democracy can fix it. Thus "the system is fair to everyone. . . . Individuals get the rewards they earn."[16] You might recognize this as a broad description of the American Dream. Whether the goals are a secure job and a chance to send your kids to college, a white picket fence and 2.3 children, or making your first million and betting it all on black, the promise of the American Dream has long been that merit will get you there or at least give you a good chance.

As a general proposition, research and polling data suggest that Americans historically do indeed accept the premises of this dominant ideology and believe we live in a meritocracy,[17] though the degree to which we believe it varies according to social and economic status, with members of racial and class groups that have been most explicitly excluded from American opportunity structures expressing the most dissent.[18] The dominant ideology is also subject to challenges from other perspectives and wanes at "crisis" moments when confidence in the American system ebbs. There is good reason to think we are living through one of those ideological crises now—the American Dream was "tainted," as Eric Mitchell told me, even before the economic and social upheaval of 2020. What's more, our answers to pollsters' questions about how our country works do not necessarily capture how that

Brooklynite thinks about her parents paying her rent, or how the Mitchell brothers ended up with such different understandings of how their lives have worked out.

YOU Didn't Build That

It seems quaint from today's perspective, but Barack Obama's "you didn't build that" remark to a hypothetical business owner during the 2012 presidential election caused a hullabaloo. There was a hashtag (#YouDidntBuildThat), a TV ad cut by the Romney campaign, and an original song by country musician Lane Turner called "I Built It" performed at the Republican National Convention, where speaker after speaker declared that actually they did build it and told stories about a rise from humble roots. People seemed to feel insulted. Here's what Obama said:

> I'm always struck by people who think, well, it must be because I was just so smart. There are a lot of smart people out there. It must be because I worked harder than everybody else. Let me tell you something—there are a whole bunch of hardworking people out there.
>
> If you were successful, somebody along the line gave you some help. There was a great teacher somewhere in your life. Somebody helped to create this unbelievable American system that we have that allowed you to thrive. Somebody invested in roads and bridges. If you've got a business—you didn't build that.[19]

Obama was addressing not just the American system but his business owner's self-image and sense of self-worth. He hit a nerve because in American culture, merit in the professional realm is closely associated with the notion of dignity.

It may not be obvious to many Americans—it was not obvious to me when I first started researching this subject—but dignity does not have to work this way. Dignity can be rooted in group or tribal associations, in castes, in religious or spiritual beliefs about human value. In some times and places, connecting dignity to work achievement, according to Richard Sennett and Jonathan Cobb, "would have seemed absurd."[20] That harvest was just a harvest, not a reflection of your worth. But in America, likely in part because of the long-standing premise that our society is organized meritocratically, professional accomplishment means something more.

Many people of high socioeconomic status draw a sense of pride from their accomplishments and social place.[21] It was this pride that Obama's comments challenged. When he said that some business owners' success had less to do with *them* than they thought, he threatened to separate them from their accomplishments, depriving them of a source of dignity. The working class and downwardly mobile, meanwhile, are often made to feel that their station is a reflection of their worth, and that they are inferior.[22] A janitor told Sennett and Cobb for their study *The Hidden Injuries of Class* that if he had been "a better person, like if I made something of myself, then people couldn't push me around,"[23] treating his perceived lack of professional success as an indicator of his value as a human.

Which is not to say that dignity corresponds directly or neatly with professional status. I will never forget cable news host and millionaire Chris Matthews, years before he resigned from MSNBC, asking, "Am I part of the winner's circle in American life? I don't think so,"[24] illustrating the tendency of some people only to compare upward, lose sight of their actual socioeconomic standing, and perhaps feel like losers in comparison to better-off friends and neighbors. And of course many working people draw a sense of dignity and pride from the belief that they are earning their way, even if they haven't climbed to the top of the social ladder.

Taking stock of your dignity—of your worth as a human— means figuring out where you stand in relation to some idea of what a person is or ought to be. In America this may not necessarily mean gauging value by economic status. But it often means grappling with the role of merit in your working life. This makes the premise that Americans live in a meritocracy a very important one for Americans to sort out.

As Americans have fought more frequently and forcefully about whether this country's system is "rigged," a number of thinkers have interrogated the premises, procedures, and flaws of American meritocracy. Two important early entries in the conversation were Chris Hayes's prescient 2012 book about the failures of America's meritocratic class, *Twilight of the Elites*, and Shamus Khan's *Privilege*, an ethnography of an elite boarding school. These were built on by Joseph Kett with his history of the notion of merit, Lani Guinier with her analysis of higher education, Phoebe Maltz Bovy with her critique of privilege discourse, and Richard Reeves with his critique of the American middle class. There have of course been numerous essays and articles revolving around the same subjects, including many prominent pieces in 2020 dealing specifically with the country's failures regarding race.[25] Often these endeavors begin from the premise that something is wrong with American meritocracy (using inequality as a jumping-off point), persuasively demonstrate that we don't live in a meritocracy at all, and propose ways to rethink and rework our social organization to correct this. A few thinkers such as Jo Littler, Daniel Markovits, and Jonathan Mijs have questioned the very premise that a real meritocracy would be a good thing. Meritocracy itself is the problem, they argue.

What was missing from this conversation, I thought, was a careful examination of how we think about merit in a personal context—of how we decide whether an individual has earned something, and whether to grant him or her the dignity associated with meritorious achievement. After all, at the heart of all our talk about mobility and inequality are the individuals whose merit is in question, whether a business owner, a computer technician, or a grocery store clerk. If we are going to rethink meritocracy as a system, we should consider how it is understood culturally and colloquially.

Asking "Did You Earn It?"

After leaving my interview with Eric, I was walking down Market Street in downtown Philadelphia when I saw a brief confrontation. About half a block ahead of me a panhandler was sitting on the sidewalk, making his pitch to passersby. A man wearing a nice suit and headphones walked past him and, as he did, turned his head and said something—I have no idea what—to the man on the ground. The panhandler became instantly enraged, half-rising from his seat on the concrete and gesturing animatedly. The man in the suit never broke stride, but I think he turned back again, briefly and without much concern, to make another comment before continuing on his way.

Again, I don't know what the man in the suit said. It could well have been something as innocent as "not today, sir." But what I imagined him to have said was something along the lines of "get a job." (A friend reading a draft of this book was surprised by my interpretation, noting "I've seen panhandlers harass people in suits a lot more than I've seen the opposite.") At the time, I was in the midst of connecting with people from a bunch of different walks of life to interview them for this project, and the incident got me thinking: I have not interviewed any assholes. The people

I was interviewing were kind to me, and by definition the sort of people willing to grant an hour to a stranger. None of them struck me as the type of person who would tell a panhandler to get a job.

I bring this up now in order to state at the outset: this project is not a definitive accounting of the understanding of merit in American life. The findings I relay and the arguments I make are limited by the size and makeup of my samples, whatever hesitancies some of my interviewees may have felt in expressing their ideas to me, and my own shortcomings as an interviewer and analyst. I don't really know what a definitive project on a subject as enormous as the American idea of merit would look like, but I think what I present here offers valuable insights about our colloquial use of the concept and some ideas about a new way to engage with it.

If you want to understand what people think about something, one of the most useful things you can do is to ask them about it. So the crux of this project is sixty in-depth interviews with Americans about their lives and how they interpret them. The individuals I interviewed are relatively diverse in terms of gender, race (though disproportionately either black or white), education, generation, occupation, and political perspective, though again, they do *not* constitute a representative sample. These were people I recruited by reaching out to potential "connectors" in various communities— a membership coordinator at a community center, the head of a political committee, a guy who organizes a pickup basketball game, etc.—and asking them for references, then asking people who spoke to me if they would refer me to a friend. The group I wound up with includes a dairy farmer, a police officer, a probation officer, a former go-go dancer, a handyman, a fireman, a teacher, a retired military intelligence officer, a computer technician, an unemployed former veterinary technician, an investor, a med student, a grocery store clerk, a drug dealer, a tech entrepreneur, a clergyman, an attorney, an EMT trainee, an office manager, a housewife, a massage therapist, and others. Interviewees met with me in their homes, in coffee shops and restaurants, and in other institutions in their communities, and spoke to me for about an hour, give or take a few minutes, depending on how much they liked to talk. The University of Pennsylvania paid them each $10 for their time. In this book, I've changed all of their names, as well as other details such as occupation or hometown where such information seemed recognizable enough to potentially enable readers to identify someone.

Most interviewees lived in and around Philadelphia; a few were from an exurban area outside the city, and a few more from the rust belt city of York, Pennsylvania. The reason for this concentration is, of course, that Philly is where I live, and it introduces the potential for some meaningful geographic bias in the stories I heard. Different regions have different cultures, and it is fair to wonder how these conversations would have sounded in Silicon Valley, in rural Arkansas, or in an immigrant community in Texas. I do think, though, that the Philadelphia region is as good as any other one place to form impressions of broader American culture, given that it is home to struggling postindustrial neighborhoods, a revitalized downtown, affluent (and less affluent) suburbs, gentrifying corridors, rural pockets, and exurban developments. You can find a lot of different American experiences around Philly, and I tried to do so.

Before digging deep into these interviews, I look closely at biographical media coverage of thirty public figures from politics, sports, and business—key sectors of American public life that set a standard for what success means and how it is achieved. Media researchers have identified meritocracy and the American Dream as important themes in a variety of different kinds of media, particularly in coverage of celebrities, whose lives often serve as parables of success that we use to understand how society and life work.[26] To grasp our colloquial understanding of merit, I wanted to examine how we explain these communally shared model lives. So I read about contemporary public figures like LeBron James, Serena Williams, Katie Ledecky, Jeb Bush, Carly Fiorina, Donald Trump, co-founder of Twitter Biz Stone, and Sheryl Sandberg. I also read about a number of broadly analogous public figures from the 1980s and 1990s, such as Michael Jordan, Steffi Graf, Jackie Joyner-Kersee, George H. W. Bush, Jesse Jackson, Mary Kay Ash, and Sam Walton. I considered how media coverage of these figures explains why they are who they are.

I am building here on work from a variety of fields. Probably the seminal relevant work, from sociology, can be found in the 1986 book *Beliefs about Inequality* by James Kluegel and Eliot Smith, which includes findings from a large-scale survey of Americans driving at questions like "Why are some Americans richer than I am? Do they work harder to succeed, or are they more talented than I am? Why are others poor: Are laziness and bad moral character primarily responsible for poverty or are lack of education and social and economic discrimination?"[27] I'll discuss findings from this work and others that drew on it throughout the book, but what I hope to add is both a timely update and a perspective that focuses on how the stories we tell help us to arrive at the conclusions we reach.

When humans make assessments and decisions, we use the "traditional rationality" of logic, evidence, and experts less than we'd like to think, wrote the communications scholar Walter Fisher.[28] Instead we use a "narrative rationality" whereby we look for "good reasons" in recognizable storylines that are culturally coherent.[29] For example, it is "coherent" for a politician to explain that he cares about the interests of working people because he grew up poor; it is not coherent for him to explain that he cares about working people because he likes apples. An explanation is not coherent because it's necessarily true. We've just learned that it makes sense.[30] In telling our own stories, we make selections from a "cultural menu" of coherent options, deploying one recognizable storyline, rejecting another, adapting a third to suit our purposes.[31]

What I did in this project was to look at the events and experiences people highlight, and the conclusions they draw about them,[32] to see what storylines they use to explain their lives and evaluate what they have earned or deserve. I did not assume events were necessarily being described to me *accurately*, nor that interpretations were given in candor, nor even that people's thoughts and opinions on these matters are consistent over time. (Indeed, I conducted interviews in which participants appeared to contradict their own stated views.) By attending to people's stories, I wanted to get a sense of what makes sense to Americans on this subject, the "good reasons" we use for assigning merit and deservedness to individual lives.

By "we"—a term I use presumptuously throughout this book—I don't mean *everyone*, and I don't mean that most Americans fit my descriptions *exactly*. What I was looking for here were the story patterns that many Americans deploy generally, and even more grapple with, as they seek to explain their lives.

I was genuinely curious and uncertain about what I would find. Would Americans play according to type and describe their working lives as essentially meritocratic? Would we reflect the contemporary social and political atmosphere, with its skepticism about our economic system? There is a famous line from two iconic American works, the Clint Eastwood film *Unforgiven* and the HBO drama *The Wire*: "Deserve's got nothing to do with it." In both cases the line is spoken by one character preparing to execute another, explaining that the world doesn't work the way the would-be victim thinks it ought to. The line is affecting because it contradicts a fundamental American pretense: that what we deserve matters. What do we actually think deserve's got to do with anything?

Flexible Merit

One important piece of the answer that I offer crystallized for me while I was talking to Nick, a twenty-eight-year-old corporate attorney. Nick liked being a lawyer. He had grown up in South Jersey, the middle child of parents who had, in his words, "white-collar jobs" but "a blue-collar work ethic." They lived in a less wealthy section of a more wealthy suburb. Nick got his undergraduate degree from a state university, working forty hours a week to pay his way. After that, he attended an elite law school, discovered a passion for contract law (!), and landed a job at a law firm with Fortune 50 clients. He said he felt successful.

When I asked Nick whether he thought he had wound up about where he deserved to be professionally, on the basis of his efforts and abilities, he said, "Yes and no." He was not sure he deserved to get into his elite law school. His LSAT scores were not especially strong, and he suspected he had been admitted because of a recommendation from a chancellor at his undergraduate school, which he regarded as something less than meritocratic. Since his entering the workplace, however, his answer to the meritocracy question was yes: he was smart, he worked hard, and so deserved his success.

But then he went on, "I have become acutely aware . . . let me take a step back. I sort of always thought it was a meritocracy, particularly the workplace. And it's not." He mentioned women at his firm, "female attorneys that I work with who I think are smarter than me," who are "just not going to be as successful." They get less desirable projects, or don't get promoted, because of the sexism of male bosses. So for him, he said, merit had been rewarded. "But I don't think that's representative."

This stopped me. I wondered: If these women Nick worked with deserved to have his job more than he did, and he and they couldn't all have the job at the same time, how could he deserve to have the job?

I don't mean that I thought Nick was wrong. It sounded to me like he had earned his position too. It was just that when you interrogated the connection between his merit and the system that was supposed to reward it, you found a pretty clear disconnect.

Nick was far from alone in this. It was startling, given Americans' reputation on this issue, how many of my interviewees thought it was *obvious* that we don't live in a functional meritocracy: about fifty out of sixty. And while I don't take this for a statistically meaningful finding, it was true across liberals and conservatives, and across people who regarded themselves as successful or unsuccessful. Interviewees whom I was confident would describe the United States as a meritocracy did not do so. For example, a sixty-nine-year-old conservative white guy who grew up poor in the heartland, cleaned oil burners, and eventually built his own successful company surprised me by saying that a lot of people don't get a fair shot. At the same time, many of the people who recognized America's unmeritocratic nature thought that *they personally* had ended up about where they deserved to be. This included individuals ranging from a young white woman who had grown up wealthy, acknowledged her considerable advantage, and concluded that she deserved her success because she used her advantages correctly, to an older unemployed black man who saw society as systematically racist but concluded that he personally deserved his lot because of specific mistakes he had made.

There are also, of course, Americans who don't think they deserve their lot. I spoke with people who think they deserve more than they've gotten from America so far, and people who said they've been lucky and probably deserve less. But what was striking about the self-identified deserves and deserve-nots was that they employed a similar logic in making their assessments. Though there are important differences among Americans in what we say about how we got to where we are—women tend to cite outside help more than men, for example—even people extremely attuned to big external factors in their lives such as race, class, gender, or the whims of the market approached the task in the same broad manner. To take stock of whether they earned their places, people grappled with circumstances, structures, luck, effort, and ability, then asked whether they had done enough on their own, given their circumstances, to merit their lot.

The reasons people offered for their own deservedness (or lack thereof) were not necessarily consistent with meritocratic standards. What we see in our stories is that, in both the ways we think about "agency" and accomplishing things on our own, and the ways we measure and grapple with the role of advantages and disadvantages in our lives, we are adept at navigating contradictions with the meritocratic ideal. Indeed, the reason Nick can conclude he earned his position despite discrimination in his workplace is that societal-level meritocracy is not his standard for deserved-ness. His standard is more personal, and it is up to him to calculate whether he meets it. Which raises questions about the precise meaning of the American Dream.

Impossible Meritocracy

When Americans argue about the American Dream, people who object to the status quo (often but not always from the left) tend to argue that meritocracy is a trick. The myth of meritocracy provides justification for huge disparities in wealth and status by suggesting that they are earned, when in fact they are not, because of nepotism, privilege, affirmative action, welfare, etc.

The flexibility in our stories shows that this critique is not quite right—or at least not the entire picture. Our ability to conclude that an individual has earned his or her position despite obvious unmeritocratic currents indicates that we are not so much deluded about meritocracy as we are hypocritical, treating meritocracy as a prerequisite for deservedness at the theoretical level but not in our actual lives. More generously, you might say that we decline to hold individuals responsible for factors out of their control. Nick the lawyer can't help it if the system is rigged; all he can do is to do a good job, and he feels this should be enough to reward himself the dignity of deservedness. Whether we're being generous or not, though, the upshot is the same: we accept outcomes as valid without even a putatively meritocratic process. This is why objections to inequality that emphasize the unmeritocratic nature of American life may miss the mark. We already know we don't live in a meritocracy, and we don't especially care.

But if our flexible notion of merit enables us to avoid living up to the meritocratic ideal, it also points the way toward really and truly rethinking that ideal. It gives us tools to reevaluate not just our execution of meritocracy but the premise itself.

Recall that Americans tend not to question *whether* we should aspire to meritocracy. Even when we're reflecting on our meritocratic system, we "cannot get our heads outside of it," the writer Helen Andrews observed in a 2016 essay about some of the recent literature on the subject. Andrews noticed that most of the thinkers who tackle the question offer fairly lukewarm ideas for reform: "None of [the authors'] remedies are more than tweaks to make the system more efficient or less prejudicial to the poor. . . . They are incapable of imagining what it would be like not to believe in it. They assume the validity of the very thing they should be questioning."[33]

My interviewees also generally stopped short of questioning meritocracy *as an ideal*. A woman named Deb, for instance, a former lawyer who works as a manager for a state agency, has thought a lot about merit and its relationship to success in America, and emerged skeptical. "There's this thing called privilege and people with privilege get farther in life," she said. "To use that simple analogy of a race, you started out ten steps ahead. You're gonna finish earlier. And if we finish at the same time, that means I'm just faster than you."

In one sense, this perspective works as a critique of American meritocracy, because Deb views our meritocracy as flawed. But more profoundly, this perspective is a *defense* of meritocratic values. The race metaphor implies that the starting line should be even, and that if it were, the results of the race would be valid. It embraces the idea that we can and should live in a meritocracy. This is a sign of a truly powerful ideology: it is able to "redefine protest in defense of the system, as a complaint about shortcomings from its ideals."[34] Meritocracy traps us: even when we think we are attacking it, we are in an important sense reinforcing its foundation. We object to American meritocracy as a *violation* of meritocracy.

But it's important to remember that there are other ways and reasons to object to the meritocratic vision. As Michael Young understood, meritocracy is an ideology of inequality even under the best of circumstances. It says that inequality is acceptable and indeed desirable if it's done right. One might object that the meritocratic arrangement is not, in fact, desirable, or ask whether the distribution of rewards according to merit is a plausible, coherent notion.

This is where Americans' flexible narrative understanding of the role of merit in our lives holds some promise. We actually understand that life is complicated, messy, and often unfair. Maybe we would be open to the idea that an individual *can't* really be isolated from his or her circumstances, or at least that we'll never get to the bottom of what merit has to do with any individual's success. Maybe we would be open to softening our commitment to the meritocratic ideal. But we would need to hear that argument more.

Again, I won't suggest that we should or could abandon the tenets of meritocracy altogether. Instead I propose that in discussions of social status and professional success, we could ask more often not just whether people are getting what we deserve, according to merit, but whether we can. If we grapple more with the possibility that when it comes to success and failure, "deserve's got nothing to do with it," it might be easier to push for the kinds of policies one might embrace if one thought meritocracy was not just unachieved but unachievable—policies that focus not merely on opportunity and mobility but on greater equality regardless of perceived deservedness.

Sneak Preview

Chapter 1 is about famous people. It shows that American culture does not take for granted the role of merit in achievement, even in the cases of successful public figures. We treat merit as an open question in each case, and attempt to answer it by taking stock of both circumstances and individual contributions. Chapter 2 considers the ways "everyday" (that is, not famous) Americans deal with circumstances such as structure and fortune in their stories. Americans are sometimes accused of not accounting for these factors in our understanding of success and failure, but I did not find this to be the case in my interviews. Americans' assessments of advantage and disadvantage are not necessarily *accurate*, but we do assess them, and this chapter shows how. Chapter 3 examines our complex and sometimes contradictory notion of *agency* by asking which aspects of their lives my interviewees considered to be under their control and which qualities they said make someone deserving. The traits and behaviors Americans say are meritorious are not actually the ones meritocracy seeks to reward, even in theory.

Chapter 4 looks at the conclusions we reach about what we have earned or deserve and the standards we use to reach them, arguing that the most common standard for deservedness Americans use is *merit* more than *meritocracy*. Chapter 5 makes the case that to challenge inequality and raise standards of living, stories and discourse about success and failure should focus less on pointing out the flawed execution of meritocracy and more on admitting that it is incoherent—that life is too complicated and arbitrary for merit to be reliably rewarded, and that what we accomplish has not much to do with what we deserve.

There is a great deal of emotional and material investment tied up in the American idea that merit can and should be rewarded in our working lives. It serves as a justification for the distribution of prestige and resources in society and informs our sense of self-worth. After talking to Americans about the role merit plays in their own lives, and reading accounts of the lives of American public figures, I think that the ways we assess merit are in many ways confused and contradictory—but also in an important sense filled with potential. We are in a moment now when, because of simmering doubts about meritocracy, interrogating our assumptions and tapping this potential seem possible. That's why this book exists.

1

American Idols

Every chance Carly Fiorina got when she was a candidate in the Republican presidential primary in 2016, the former Hewlett-Packard head told audiences that she had gone "from secretary to CEO." She used the line in stump speeches and debates. She bought the URL fromsecretarytoceo.com. Fiorina also called herself "self-made" and claimed that her story was possible "only in America." The imagery was at the core of her candidacy.

Then a curious thing happened. The *Washington Post*'s Fact Checker published a column slapping Fiorina with a "three Pinocchio" rating for her secretary-to-CEO claim.[1] Three Pinocchios, according to the *Post*, indicates a claim that contains "significant factual error and/or obvious contradictions." Such claims are "mostly false" but "could include statements which are technically correct (such as based on official government data) but are so taken out of context as to be very misleading." The *Post* chose this rating despite verifying that Fiorina had in fact worked as a secretary before she became a CEO.

The problem with Fiorina's claim, wrote Fact Checker reporter Michelle Ye Hee Lee, is that "it evokes a rags-to-riches-esque narrative. . . . Fiorina uses a familiar, 'mailroom to boardroom' trope of upward mobility that the public is familiar with, yet her story is nothing like that." The candidate, the *Post* explained, was the daughter of Joseph Sneed, who was a prominent attorney, a federal judge, a deputy attorney general in the Nixon administration, and the dean of Duke University School of Law. Fiorina attended Stanford, where her tuition likely was paid in full by Duke as part of her father's compensation. Though she worked a number of secretarial jobs during and after college, "she always intended to attend graduate school for her career." Fiorina had not hidden or denied these facts, but, the *Post* argued, she told an "only-in-America" story despite enjoying many "only-for-Fiorina" opportunities.

The column set off a mini-firestorm. On Fox News, Howard Kurtz called the piece a "misfire" (he awarded the paper "four Pinocchios").[2] Fiorina said the story "sort of floored me,"[3] and on social media and in the paper's comments section, readers sounded off. Partly the conflagration was about whether evoked narratives should be the province of fact checkers. But partly it was about the validity of Fiorina's claims and the *Post*'s critique.

Those who sided with the *Post* argued that Fiorina's class background disqualified her from self-made status and from the "rags-to-riches" trajectory they thought she had claimed. Her rise had not been *unlikely*, they said, which meant it didn't match what she was describing. Several went further and suggested that the candidate's success had been largely predetermined by her socioeconomic advantages. She was "bound for some kind of top-tier job practically from the cradle," wrote the blogger Kevin Drum at *Mother Jones*.[4] A commenter named Claire Sparks on the *Post*'s website argued, "If we all had parents who could get us all free rides to an Ivy League school, we could all be CEOs."[5]

Among Fiorina's defenders, some contended that the candidate's advantages had not been as great as her critics suggested.

"Being the daughter of a law professor, or of a law school dean, hardly puts her in the .0001%. Upper middle class at most," wrote another *Post* commenter named BurbankBob. Others argued that Fiorina's socioeconomic edge was neutralized by her gender disadvantage. "There is one important reality that is lost on Ms. Lee," wrote the commenter Lee Pelletier. "Women who came of age in the 70s faced very tough odds, including those who were daughters of power."[6]

Finally, some of Fiorina's defenders resisted the suggestion that the candidate's achievements could or should be contextualized in relation to her family at all. "This article is an absolute joke," an Ohio county commissioner named Brian Stewart tweeted at the *Washington Post.*[7] "She was a secretary, and she became a CEO, but you call her a liar bc her dad was lawyer." In a post at the conservative site NewsBusters, Tom Blumer wrote: "The candidate isn't claiming rags-to-riches. . . . She's claiming that she worked hard, and smart, and took advantage of the opportunities presented."[8]

Whether or not Fiorina implied that she rose from rags to riches, she clearly meant to suggest that she had risen up the ranks of American society through merit. And so it's worth noting the extent to which her claim was *not* accepted at face value. Many observers, including people with prominent mainstream media platforms, openly questioned whether Fiorina's success was the product of a meritocratic process. Nor is this phenomenon unique to Carly Fiorina. It is actually rather astounding, given Americans' reputation for believing that we live in a meritocracy, how often we reject or question this premise when thinking and talking about the people at the top.

In this chapter I make the case that even in instances of extreme achievement—the paragons, the winners, the people whose merit should be most obvious and who have long been understood as symbols of meritocracy—American culture tends to debate or evaluate the role of merit in success rather than accept it. I'll take a look at how we argue about whether people like Carly Fiorina deserve to be where they are and ask what our uncertainty about the Big Shots means for the rest of us.

Triumph of the Mass Idols

In 1944 a sociologist named Leo Lowenthal published a paper examining "biographies" of public figures from two mainstream American magazines, *Collier's* and the *Saturday Evening Post*. Lowenthal was a German refugee and a member of the "Frankfurt School" of theorists who became known for (among other things) turning a critical eye toward the mass culture they encountered in the United States, identifying in it some of the indoctrinating qualities they had witnessed under fascism. Lowenthal argued that these magazine biographies, which we would now call profiles, had changed over time. Around the turn of the twentieth century, the bios had focused on "idols of production," major figures from the worlds of politics and business, and presented them as "examples of success which can be imitated." Biographies from around the early 1940s were more frequently about "idols of consumption," major figures from the worlds of sports and entertainment. For these latter heroes, success was portrayed as "an accidental and irrational event," the result of lucky breaks. Lowenthal dubbed this evolution the "triumph of the mass idols" and viewed it as a symptom of societal decline.[9]

The idea that American media portray success as accidental didn't stick. But in making his argument, Lowenthal embraced a premise that has proved resonant: the idols of a society reflect its socioeconomic conditions, as well as the ways people *think and feel* about those conditions.[10] That is to say, the stories we tell about public figures reveal and reinforce the public's sense of how society works at any given time, and specifically the question of who succeeds and why. Of course, other kinds of stories beyond the life stories of famous people reflect these cultural tenets too, and meritocracy is a theme in myriad genres of American narrative. The nineteenth-century author Horatio Alger became so well known for his fictional stories about characters rising from humble roots that his name remains shorthand for tales of self-made success. Hollywood movies,[11] reality television,[12] sitcoms,[13] and news stories[14] have all been analyzed for their portrayal—and usually boosterism—of American meritocracy. The theme is not hard to find. *The Little Engine That Could* teaches children that if they work hard, anything is possible. But for explanations of success and failure, nonfiction portrayals of celebrities and public figures have remained of particular interest to cultural analysts.[15]

Fiorina, for example, was joining a long, if not especially proud, tradition among presidential candidates in spinning her meritocratic tale. In a study of presidential campaign films, which introduce candidates to the broad public at national party conventions, media critic Joanne Morreale observes that in the biographical portions of the films, "candidates often come from humble beginnings, but work hard to become successful. Whenever possible, they are described as poor, although hard work, determination, and commitment to education enables them to succeed. The candidates conform to the American ideal of success embodied by the rags-to-riches, Horatio Alger myth. The individual who strives to achieve can overcome economic hardships."[16]

From Abraham Lincoln's being born in a log cabin to Barack Obama's being raised by a single mother, candidates who could credibly point back to the humble roots from whence they came have done so, emphasizing the role of merit in their rise. Similar stories get told about rich people who *aren't* running for president. The yarns spun about business leaders and entrepreneurs are frequently driven by the "self-made myth," the notion "that individual and business success is the result of personal characteristics of exceptional individuals, such as hard work, creativity, and sacrifice, with little or no outside assistance."[17]

Star athletes and entertainers—Lowenthal's idols of consumption—can serve as models of advancement through merit too. Cultural critics have identified sports heroes as common and effective vehicles for lessons about meritocracy. Sport, writes Michael Serazio, "consistently embeds a narrative that explains achievement in terms of meritocracy. Winners succeed, sports tell us, because they work hard."[18] Athletes as distant in time and context as Babe Ruth and Michael Jordan were presented as examples of the American Dream and the authors of their own success.[19] Entertainers have also been molded by the iconographers who write about them to embody the self-made ideal. Reading coverage from celebrity magazines across the twentieth century, the sociologist Karen Sternheimer finds the American Dream surfacing as a theme throughout.[20]

The implication of this kind of story, most analysts agree, is that America is a meritocracy, or at least close enough. Celebrity stories suggest that "upward mobility is possible in America" and "inequality is the result of personal failure rather than systematic social conditions."[21] The sports narratives, by foregrounding hard work, "assure those who lack [athletic] talents—the vast majority of people—that they too can succeed,"[22] and foster the illusion that "one day, the 'ordinary but special' individual consumer may realize his or her unique qualities, and join the ever-changing pantheon of celebrities."[23] The lesson we take, that winners "must have risen to the top through fair means and thus deserve their position," writes Susan Birrell, is "insidious": it encourages us to accept and support inequality.[24]

This does not mean, necessarily, that the stories fool us so much as that they invite us to "collude" with the meritocratic fantasy, as Sternheimer explains it. "The myth of mobility makes Americans feel good about ourselves and is woven into our sense of nationalism."[25]

There's a great deal that these analyses get right about American culture and the pervasiveness of messages about meritocracy. But I'm going to argue that it's important to note how conversations about high achievers also regularly grapple with the possibility of unmeritocratic outcomes. In published stories of the lives of politicians, business magnates, and star athletes, meritocracy is less consistently constructed as a societal *reality* than as an *ideal*. Again, a former CEO and presidential candidate was called a liar by one of the most prestigious news outlets in the country for saying she rose from secretary to CEO. An individual's merit is an open question in American culture, and we ought to consider how we answer it.

"Why Should He Even Be There?": Meritocracy in Politics

The first recorded biographical campaign literature in American politics was distributed by Andrew Jackson, and its themes, if not its particulars, would be familiar today: Jackson was portrayed as a simple "soldier-farmer," both a man of the people and a hero of two wars.[26] This everyman understood and empathized with voters, and had proven his exceptional ability by rising from a low station to a high one, Jackson's boosters said. It was classic meritocratic material. He was just like you, only better.

Jackson's opponents pushed back, however, noting that "Old Hickory" was a slaveholder who hadn't really worked the land, and that he had been thirteen at the time of the first war in which he claimed to have fought. Ever since, for every candidate who claims meritorious achievements, there have been journalists, opponents, and voters who analyze and often reject those claims—in the process making implicit and explicit arguments about how success works in America and what merit has to do with it.

To get a sense of these arguments, I looked closely at media coverage and campaign content dealing with candidates' biographies from two presidential elections, 1988 and 2016. I chose these elections in part because I wanted to see whether the notion of merit was treated differently before and after the global financial crash of 2008, and in part because neither election involved an incumbent, which meant there were multiple viable candidates from both parties seeking to introduce themselves and their life stories to voters. I tried to use the same types of materials from each campaign: journalistic profiles from the major outlets of the time, candidate bios from brochures (1988) and campaign websites (2016), campaign speeches and advertisements. I considered the explanations offered and arguments made about why the candidates got to where they were in life.

What I found was that even in 1988, American political discourse was very much open to the possibility that its most prominent figures were *not* products of meritocracy—that there were other ways people could reach the top. By 2016, the skepticism of the eighties would seem mild.

1988

George H. W. Bush, the incumbent vice president and front-runner for the 1988 Republican presidential nomination, had been born rich—his father had been a banker and US senator—while his strongest challenger in the Republican primary, Bob Dole, had not. Dole hailed from the absurdly heartland town of Russell, Kansas, where his father ran a creamery and his mother sold sewing machines, and the family struggled through the Great Depression. Neither the political press nor Dole left this difference unremarked upon. Dole announced his candidacy in Russell. On the stump, he went on "at practiced length about his dust-bowl youth in the outback town"[27] and told audiences he was a "product of 'public schools' who didn't 'start at the top.'"[28]

The implications were clear, but Dole spelled them out anyway. Speaking about his background to the *Washington Post*, Dole said: "I didn't dream it up to go after Bush. . . . But it's true. He started at the top and he stayed there. That says something. . . . Why should he even be there?"[29] Elsewhere, Dole claimed that Americans wanted "someone in the White House who got there the hard way."[30] Meanwhile, the *Post* speculated that Bush had a "Silver Spoon problem."[31]

Both Dole and the press, in other words, suggested that Bush's wealthy origins could have been responsible for his success. By doing so, they allowed that life *can* and sometimes *does* work this way in America. Bush would, of course, go on to win the primary and eventually the presidency. But the critique was politically potent enough that he had to deal with it onstage at the Republican National Convention. Accepting his nomination, he said:

> Yes, my parents were prosperous, and their children were lucky. But there were lessons we had to learn about life. . . . And I learned a few things about life in a place called Texas.

And when I was working on this part of the speech, Barbara came in and asked what I was doing, and I looked up and I said, "I'm working hard." And she said, "Oh, dear, don't worry. Relax, sit back, take off your shoes and put up your silver foot."

Now, we moved to west Texas 40 years ago, 40 years ago this year. The war was over, and we wanted to get out and make it on our own. Those were exciting days. We lived in a little shotgun house, one room for the three of us. Worked in the oil business and then started my own.[32]

"*Yes, my parents were prosperous, and their children were lucky. But . . .* Bush indicates that he earned his station, but feels compelled in doing so to explain that he struck out on his own, away from his parents. He is on the defensive.

Bush was dealing with the same fundamental issue the *Post* would raise almost thirty years later about Fiorina: a person does not earn his or her class of origin, and Americans understand implicitly that rich kids have a head start. In fact, while candidates' harping on their humble roots has rightly been interpreted as conveying the message that mobility is *possible* in America, it simultaneously conveys an understanding that steep upward trajectories are impressive. American political culture reflects the imperfection of our meritocracy in this regard, if not the statistical reality that dramatic mobility is highly unlikely. This is certainly not to say that coming from a wealthy or prominent background *hampers* candidates like Bush. The practical advantages of name, network, etc. clearly outweigh the drawbacks. But skepticism about the merit of such politicians has long been a part of American political culture.

Nor is class background the only reason used in American politics for doubting a candidate's merit. On the Democratic side in 1988, Jesse Jackson ran a strong insurgent primary campaign.

A minister who rose to prominence in the civil rights movement, Jackson made very clear that he hadn't been gifted a position of prominence in American society because of class. "I was not supposed to make it. You see, I was born of a teenage mother, who was born of a teenage mother," said Jackson. The press occasionally pushed back on this. An article in the *New York Times Magazine* noted: "Neither the Haynie Street area, where [Jackson] was born, nor the other Greenville [South Carolina] neighborhoods he lived in later were what would be called slums, his relatives and childhood friends say today. They remember a comfortable home, better than most, a freezer on the porch and plenty of food around for his visiting friends."[33] But having had a freezer was an insufficient explanation for rising to national political prominence, and Jackson's opponents and the press mostly accepted that the candidate had, in fact, achieved prominence because he was talented and driven. That did not mean, however, that they said he deserved it.

Over and over, journalists writing profiles of Jackson and the sources they quoted referred to Jackson's "gifts" as a communicator,[34] and his "enormous innate sense of the media."[35] They also noted his ambition and work ethic. "Everybody knew that only the strivers could overcome segregation and racism," wrote Gail Sheehy in a psychologically focused profile.[36] But they questioned his motivation. Some suggested the candidate was driven by insecurity. "I think being born out of wedlock bothered him disproportionately to the way it did anyone else we grew up with. The thing that drives him is a subliminal longing for respect and recognition," the *New York Times* quoted Jackson's brother as saying.[37]

Consequently, Jackson was accused of applying a very particular kind of effort centered on the acquisition of attention. "Detractors

say that [Jackson's] soaring words are rarely matched by deeds—
that he gets the headlines, but does not do the groundwork,"
observed a piece in the *New York Times Magazine*.[38] And according to *Newsweek*, "For years, the rap against Jackson has been his
image as a cynical opportunist, willing to do almost anything to
get ahead."[39] A key anecdote used repeatedly to convey this point
was that Jackson had falsely claimed to have cradled a dying
Martin Luther King Jr. in his arms.[40] He was called "demagogic"
and portrayed as dishonest and unserious. In short, what the press
was saying was that the candidate's *negative* qualities contributed
to his success. Jackson succeeded because of Jackson, but not because of merit.

Occasionally Jackson was also the subject of what might be
called an "affirmative action critique." In Democratic politics,
some coverage implied, being black registered as an advantage.
Time magazine noted rival candidate Michael Dukakis's "deep
reluctance to directly confront Jackson, a black man,"[41] while
George Will declared that "Jackson has had it two ways for too
long. He complains that the media treat him as a 'black candidate.'
Yet he insists that his achievements not be weighed on the same
scale that measures the achievements of white candidates."[42] This
critique was not as central as the characterological one—which is
not to dismiss the role of racism in the response to Jackson. There
is a pattern of black people's abilities being treated as unmeritori-
ous in American culture, as I'll discuss in more detail later, and
that dynamic was likely at work here.

Jackson ultimately lost the primary to Dukakis, the governor
of Massachusetts and a son of Greek immigrants who sold himself as the realization of a multigenerational American Dream.
Dukakis's father arrived in the United States speaking no
English and wound up at Harvard Medical School, while his

mother went to Bates and became a teacher, as Dukakis repeated many times during the campaign. It is interesting, from a meritocratic perspective, that Dukakis focused as much as he did on his *parents'* humble roots. The candidate often implied that he had absorbed the values and shared the experience of coming from modest means, even if he had not actually done so himself. "Discipline was strict. Lots of chores. We always earned our own spending money. Life was comfortable but by no means lavish," Dukakis said.[43]

When Dukakis met George Bush in the general election, Bush mostly left Dukakis's upbringing alone. Instead, in addition to race-baiting with his "Willie Horton" ads and making fun of Dukakis for looking silly poking out of a military tank, Bush's campaign argued that the economic turnaround Dukakis had overseen as governor was due to the decisions of Dukakis's (Republican) predecessor and improvements in the national economy under the Reagan administration. "The national economic recovery—[Dukakis's] opposition to the Reagan–Bush Administration recovery program is well-documented—benefited every governor elected in 1982," argued Bush's economic adviser Michael Boskin.[44] In other words, the Bush campaign claimed that Dukakis simply had good timing. He had *lucked into* his political success.

In the election of 1988, then, Americans heard politicians tell stories that portrayed America as a meritocracy—when they talked about themselves. But the election discourse at large hardly treated the reward of merit as a foregone conclusion in American life. Rather, when candidates spoke about their opponents and when the press examined their campaign biographies, voters heard suggestions that some people get ahead because of structural advantage, some succeed through cynicism, and some people just plumb luck out.

2016

By 2016, a much more diverse and fragmented political media, the aftermath of the Great Recession, and insurgent movements within both major parties meant that presidential candidates' claims of merit were received with even more scrutiny than before. In fact, in 2016 there was a strong sense in mainstream political discourse that merit might be *inversely* correlated with success.

I don't want to spend too much time on Jeb Bush here or anywhere else, but suffice to say that the onetime Republican front-runner's campaign was best summed up by *The Onion* in an infographic that described Bush's "Greatest Liability" this way: "O, what fickle hand of fate! 'Tis the very same privileged background that elevated him to such prominence in the first place!"[45] If opponents and the press had been wary about Bush Sr.'s wealthy roots, they often dismissed his second son entirely. No one believed Jeb was there because of Jeb.

Hillary Clinton made for a more interesting and historically significant case. Clinton was, like Jeb Bush, a legacy candidate, and though this came up now and again, it was not the focus of the conversation around her. Clinton told a meritocratic story about herself: she had worked hard, persevered through adversity, and, as a result, risen high. But in the Democratic primary she faced an opponent who rejected many traditional meritocratic premises.

Bernie Sanders said Clinton was "unqualified" despite her many conventional qualifications. More remarkably, he told reporters that his *own* rise to prominence was incidental to his presidential aspirations. ("When I asked Sanders a question about his early years, he sighed with the air of a man who knows he can no longer put off that visit to the periodontist.")[46] In so doing, he resisted weaving a standard meritocratic tale of his own. Sanders's campaign website initially provided only the most rudimentary biographical information. Eventually it was updated to include an "interactive timeline," but that timeline was not exactly a catalog of merit finding just reward. In it Sanders opposes the Defense of Marriage Act, but it passes. He opposes the second invasion of Iraq, but the United States goes to war. He pushes an amendment to prevent the government from obtaining library records on Americans, but the amendment is removed in "backroom negotiations."

Over and over in Sanders's story, Sanders is right, others are wrong, he fails to persuade them, and bad things follow. The implication is that merit gets you nowhere; the people who succeed in politics do so in spite of, or perhaps because of, corrupt values and calamitous plans. Success is cause for suspicion.

This perspective made Sanders a frustrating foil for Clinton and her supporters, who cited Clinton's occupancy of several high-ranking positions as her main qualifications for the presidency. Things would only get harder for the former secretary of state in the general election.

Donald Trump is actually a complicated figure when it comes to meritocratic rhetoric. As a candidate, he sung his own praises constantly, of course, celebrating his money, his buildings, his ratings, his polling, etc. He suggested that these successes were because of *him*, that he earned them. But it's important to note that Trump rarely celebrates the *process* of succeeding in America. "I always said winning is somewhat, maybe, innate," Trump has said when asked to explain his triumphs.[47] The ghostwriter of Trump's book *Art of the Deal*, Tony Schwartz, told *The New Yorker* that during interviews, "Trump seemed to remember almost nothing of his youth, and made it clear that he was bored" when asked about it.[48] Trump doesn't celebrate America and its meritocratic system. Trump celebrates only Trump.

This leaves plenty of room to wonder how Trump thinks everyone *else* in American politics got to where they are, and Trump usually has some theories other than "they earned it." In the 2016 Republican primary, he cast his opponents as a bunch of pathetic losers and failures who had achieved prominence for a variety of bad reasons. When he reached the general election, Trump argued that Hillary Clinton had succeeded because she was "crooked," because she played "the women's card" when "she has got nothing else going on,"[49] and, most profoundly, because the system that rewarded her was "rigged." The conservative press echoed these arguments, projecting loudly into mainstream American discourse the implication that American politicians were *anything but* the products of a properly functioning meritocracy. Trump's victory suggests that this message resonated.

During a Republican primary debate in September 2015, former governor of Arkansas Mike Huckabee made the following observation:

> I've been listening to everybody on the stage and there is a lot of back-and-forth about "I'm the only one who has done this, the only one who has done that, I've done great things."
> We've all done great things or we wouldn't be on this stage.[50]

This has not proved to be a consensus view in presidential politics. The political discourse of 1988 reflected an awareness that in America, success is sometimes determined less by merit than by class, by luck, or by dishonorable behavior. By 2016 this skepticism had turned to cynicism, and success itself had turned suspect.

Politics, of course, are inherently combative. We expect participants to tear each other down. But our uncertainty about meritocracy runs deep enough that even in accounts in which successful individuals explain their *own* success, they wrestle with questions about the role of merit. Consider, for example, the autobiographies of business magnates.

"Certainly Luck Plays a Part. But . . .": Meritocracy in Business

"In business, as in life, nothing is ever handed to you," writes Ivanka Trump, absurdly, at the start of her 2010 book *The Trump Card*. But then—and this is important—she immediately starts playing defense.[51] "That might sound like a line coming from someone with a backstory like mine. . . . Yes, I've had the great good fortune to be born into a life of wealth and privilege, with a name to match. Yes, I've had every opportunity, every advantage. And yes, I've chosen to build my career on a foundation built by my father and grandfather, so I can certainly see why an outsider might dismiss my success in our family business as yet another example of nepotism."

She assures her readers that she and her brothers "didn't rise to our positions in the company by any kind of birthright or foregone conclusion," and then instructs everyone to "get over it. Go ahead and bring it up if you feel you must. Acknowledge the elephant in the room. But then move on. Move on, because I'm way past it. Move on, because even though those who believe that my success is a result of nepotism might be right, they might also be wrong."

After this long spiel meant to put the issue of privilege behind her, Trump moves on to say, "So I've had a bit of an edge getting in the door, but that doesn't mean I haven't developed an edge of my own now that I'm all the way in the room"; "Have I had an advantage? Absolutely"; "Forget the silver spoon and the storybook upbringing"; "I'm fully aware of the favorable hand I've drawn in life."

She is not over it.

It is true that the American understanding of wealth is driven by the "self-made myth," the notion "that individual and business success is the result of personal characteristics of exceptional individuals," as Brian Miller and Mike Lapham write in a critique of self-made stories.[52] But wealthy people seeking to connect themselves to this myth often engage with critiques of American meritocracy in ways that reveal a complex relationship with the notion of "self-made." Magnates acknowledge roles for luck and structures in their lives, and defend against questions others might raise about whether those factors determined their success. The solution these moneybags tend to settle on for resolving these questions is *not* to defend the American system as reliably meritocratic so much as to assert the capacity of the exceptional individual to matter more than unfair external and systemic factors.

Ivanka Trump makes for an extreme example of this because the role her family played in her life was so obvious and profound, but she is by no means alone. I read autobiographies of six business leaders: in addition to *The Trump Card* there was *Iacocca* (1984), by the automobile executive Lee Iacocca; *Sam Walton: Made in America* (1992), by the founder of Walmart; *Mary Kay: Miracles*

Happen (1981, by the cosmetics titan Mary Kay Ash); *Things a Little Bird Told Me* (2014), by Biz Stone, co-founder of Twitter; and *Lean In* (2013), by Facebook COO Sheryl Sandberg. Sandberg's book is not a memoir, but it draws on the tech titan's life experiences.

These are very different people who project very different identities: Ash portrays herself as a prayerful woman who lives by the golden rule, Stone as the Silicon Valley innovator enamored of creativity and change, Sandberg as the technocratic executive, etc. And yet these figures have more in common than swollen bank accounts. In their books the authors (or their ghostwriters) begin from the premise that they are examples who can be emulated, then explain how they navigated unmeritocratic currents.

The typical magnate does not consider himself or herself to be especially smart or talented—or at least won't say so. "I've seen a lot of guys who are smarter than I am," writes Iacocca.[53] "I'm not a genius," promises Stone.[54] "When I was successful, it wasn't because I was more talented than the next salesperson," writes Ash.[55] "And yet," writes Iacocca, readying himself to articulate the central implicit question of most millionaire memoirs, "I've lost [the smarter guys] in the smoke. Why?"[56]

A few of the authors say they have some *other* special something besides smarts. For Iacocca, it's what he calls "horse sense," which appears to include components of decisiveness, risk-taking, seeing the big picture, and people skills. For Stone, it is optimism and creativity, combined with a willingness to take chances. Walton emphasizes his passion to compete. It can be confusing to try to sort through why these qualities, which the authors have typically displayed since early on in their lives, don't count as exceptional talents. Why is someone who is better at math than Lee Iacocca "smarter" than the auto executive if Iacocca has better horse sense? Why doesn't Stone's self-diagnosed predisposition toward creative solutions amount to a kind of genius?

In any case, these special abilities are not the focus of the cases the authors make for themselves. Instead, they explain that they succeeded because they responded to chance the right way.

Some of these rich people grew up poor. Iacocca comes down with rheumatic fever. Walton loses his first store. Stone struggles through unemployment. Ash flounders after a tough divorce. Time and again these winners suffer losses, most of which are just bad luck. Time and again their response is to persevere. They survive poverty and illness and toughen up as a result. They get back on the horse after falling off. "We fail forward to success," Ash writes. "If we ever decide to compare knees, you're going to find that I have more scars than anyone in the room. That's because I have fallen down and gotten up so many times in my life."[57]

The authors acknowledge good fortune, too. Ivanka Trump discusses her head start, as we've seen. Walton gets $20,000 from his father-in-law. Sandberg finds good mentors who help her along. In their discussions of these experiences, though, the authors don't just say that they've been lucky. They explain what they did to put themselves in position to be lucky—how they made their own luck by aggressively taking risks or following their passions—and how they acted to seize the moment. In other words, they emphasize the role of agency in interaction with luck.

These "self-made" stories do not deny or ignore luck, chance, or help. Rather, the storytellers acknowledge external factors and perform a sort of narrative judo to turn them into individual responsibility. You face bad luck, you persevere. You need good luck, you give yourself chances and seize the moment. There's a kind of quasi-statistical logic at play: Things may not always go your way, but if you take the right steps, they probably eventually will.

As for what happens after you seize the moment, well, that's not precisely meritocratic either. When the business leaders discuss their enormous wealth, they don't argue that the market pays people what they deserve. They instruct readers to fight for every last penny. Sandberg, for example, writes that women tend not to be paid what they are worth, and encourages them to negotiate more aggressively. This is not the perspective of someone who believes she lives in a smoothly functioning meritocracy.

There is an understanding throughout these books that merit and reward do not run in parallel. Sandberg's argument is built on the premise that American meritocracy includes structural unfairness in the form of discrimination against women. Ash, Trump, and Iacocca all recognize this as well. (Iacocca says his secretary would have been a vice president "if it weren't for the [male] chauvinism built into the system.") Iacocca also cites discrimination against Italians and Jews. With the exception of Walton, these writers do not particularly defend or valorize American capitalism. What they do is argue that individuals can overcome the flaws of an imperfect system. Meritocratic achievement is less like a victory in a fairly refereed sporting event than like surviving in the wilderness. You do what you have to do in the situation you encounter without concerning yourself too much with whether the situation is fair.

Strangely, several of the businesspeople proceed to the conclusion that truly, profoundly meritorious people *cannot* fail. Iacocca argues that people who appear to have done everything right— "the go-getters who followed a plan, went to school, got a good job, worked hard"—but still don't succeed must be screwing up somehow. "When you speak to these guys, they'll often tell you that they've had some bad breaks or perhaps a boss who didn't like them. Invariably, they present themselves as victims. But you have to wonder why they had only bad breaks and why they never seemed to look for good ones. Certainly luck plays a part. But a major reason capable people fail to advance is that they don't work well with their colleagues."[58]

Ash laments that most people "never dare to try. . . . Women, especially, have so much potential they never tap." If the individual approaches obstacles the correct way, success is guaranteed. "Remember that whatever you *vividly* imagine, *ardently* desire, *sincerely* believe, and *enthusiastically* act upon must *inevitably* come to pass."[59]

The authors do not consider that individuals might be operating within a system without the possibility of operating outside of it, so that even a person who does everything right could fail to surmount obstacles. (Sandberg comes the closest by acknowledging in an early caveat that "it seems like I am letting our institutions off the hook.")[60] Nor do these winners imagine that America might dole out rewards arbitrarily, or even systematically reward *negative* behaviors or attributes.

But their efforts to establish the role of merit in their own success, and to associate themselves with the "self-made myth," are not first and foremost a celebration of functional meritocracy. They describe themselves as people who triumph over American systems rather than flourish within them, and treat individual contributions to success as something to be assessed rather than assumed.

"There's Something Else in Him": Meritocracy in Sports

Sports are different from most of the rest of American life. The results are less subject to debate, the participants more obviously qualified for their roles. One might question whether Hillary Clinton was the right person for the job of secretary of state between 2009 and 2013, but it would be absurd to question whether Serena Williams should have a high seed in the US Open. This does not mean, however, that we necessarily accept sports as a meritocracy pure and simple. Google "LeBron James genetic lottery" or "overpaid athletes" and you'll see immediately that Americans are less than fully convinced that athletes *deserve* the success they enjoy. As with politicians and businesspeople, when we talk about athletes, we ask why they are where they are and what merit has to do with it.

One of the contexts in which these questions get asked most explicitly is in the sort of journalistic profiles Leo Lowenthal studied—biographical portraits that seek to explain the essence of a person. I examined at least one and usually several profiles of twelve major star athletes: Michael Jordan, Don Mattingly, Steffi Graf, Jackie Joyner-Kersee, Larry Bird, and Mike Tyson from the 1980s and 1990s, and LeBron James, Mike Trout, Serena Williams, Katie Ledecky, Stephen Curry, and Conor McGregor from more recent years. These athletes come from a diverse set of backgrounds, represent several major sports, and have occupied the media spotlight at different times, across forty years. What they share in common is undeniable superstardom, and—in the estimation of major media outlets such as *Sports Illustrated, Esquire,* and *ESPN The Magazine*—something special *beyond* physical talent.

Business leaders, you will recall, denied that outsize talent had led to their success. Journalists writing about star athletes do not typically deny that their subjects have elite innate abilities. See how Rick Telander presents Michael Jordan as a physical marvel bordering on the miraculous in a 1986 profile: "Breathes there a human anywhere who can float longer than the 23-year-old, 6'6", 200-pound Jordan? Someday an updraft will catch him in midglide, or Tinker Bell herself will sprinkle him with fairy dust, and he will waft on over the basket and up into the wires and lights of an NBA arena like a raptor soaring into the clouds."[61]

More common than this kind of florid language are matter-of-fact descriptions of the particular physical capacities deemed relevant to an athlete's performance. Mike Trout's "home runs come from his natural strength; the batting average comes from his remarkable speed."[62] According to a 1986 profile Don Mattingly "has an exceptionally quick first step for both defense and baserunning. He couldn't have only 10 more strikeouts (76) than homers (66) the last two years without great hand-eye coordination and bat speed."[63] Mike Tyson as a child was "big for his age, with enormous natural power."[64]

Occasionally a profile will focus more on physical limitations than assets. To read coverage of basketball great Larry Bird, you would think he was overweight and clubfooted: "Bird looks like a soft, fleshy adolescent. He is slow as NBA players go, and in the words of an NBA scout—not the only one who thought Bird would be a mediocre pro—he suffers from 'white man's disease.' That is, he can't jump."[65] The theme of whiteness as a physical disadvantage comes up repeatedly: "Lightning-quick black athletes . . . are the league leaders in steals . . . except for Bird."[66]

This lack of athleticism is supposed to speak well of Bird, and there's a reason for that. Though many physical capabilities can be developed and enhanced, physicality is often treated in these profiles as unearned. One profile of Bird is actually called "Gifts That God Didn't Give." If merit means "positive qualities deserving of reward," physical talent is not meritorious because, though it's a positive quality that can *lead to* reward, it does not make one deserving. This is part of the reason why the frequent attribution of black athletes' successes to sheer physical talent is racist.[67] Athletic talent is understood to be a gift rather than something earned.

Consequently, these generally complimentary profiles deliver their compliments not by celebrating athletes' physical talents but by looking beyond them. After reading a few of the pieces, I began to notice a sentence or paragraph construction that surfaced repeatedly. It said, effectively, *"yes, there are physical considerations, but . . ."* A few examples:

- *On Katie Ledecky:* "Strength, stroke efficiency and aerobic capacity all help make champions, but none of those is what separates Ledecky from her rivals."[68]
- *On Trout:* "Physically, Trout's success is simple: The home runs come from his natural strength; the batting average comes from his remarkable speed; and the overall performance comes from his ability to stay short with his swing and lay off pitches outside the strike zone. But Trout is also . . ."[69]
- *On Bird:* "Larry Bird was blessed with his height, but . . ."[70]
- *On Jackie Joyner-Kersee:* "The most convenient explanation would be purely physical . . ."[71]
- *On Mattingly:* "Part of that is talent, of course, but another part can be attributed to . . ."[72]
- *On Conor McGregor:* "The hardest hitters usually have long arms, which McGregor does, and they usually have big fists, which McGregor does, but there's something else in him . . ."[73]

Over and over these stories tell us, *there's something else* in star athletes that truly separates them from their peers and makes them deserving of stardom.

So what's the "something else"?

The propagandistic parable of Michael Jordan's rise to greatness is probably the closest thing American culture offers to a template for a story of athletic success. Jordan is cut from his high school team, and he is devastated. But "Michael worked harder than ever, growing four inches and improving dramatically over the next two years," as the narrator says in the 1989 promotional biopic *Come Fly with Me*. Aside from the apparent suggestion that Jordan willed himself to grow taller, the legend of Michael Jordan is that he overcame adversity with hard work and determination.

This of course sounds like the classic American formula for success. But although braving adversity and working hard come up a great deal in athlete profiles, neither is consistently treated as true, distinguishing merit.

Don't get me wrong—adversity is a frequent point of emphasis in tales of athletic success. Some stars, like LeBron James, Mike Tyson, and Bird, struggle by growing up poor. Serena Williams struggles under her father's strict tutelage, and later with sexism and racism in the tennis world.

Other stories stretch a little further to find a struggle in the athlete's past. A profile of Stephen Curry makes a case that his skills were developed on a rickety court at his grandparents' house in the woods of Virginia: "It's hard to get rattled by Grizzlies fans once you've hit 100 free throws in a row with actual underfed bears lurking just beyond the tree line."[74] Curry is the son of NBA star Dell Curry; his home court growing up was a well-paved driveway (which the story mentions, with considerably less emphasis), where he undoubtedly spent more time and hoisted more shots than he did at his grandfather's bear-infested property. But the story shoehorns him into a narrative of hardship.

Conor McGregor's disadvantageous experience comes from having a punchable face: "I seem to have a face—I seem to attract attention somehow," McGregor says. "For some reason, people want to try to come at me. They want to hit me. I just wanted people to leave me alone, basically."[75] Mike Trout's amusing disadvantage, identified in a profile in *GQ*, is hailing from New Jersey, where "the slushy cold has historically put a ceiling on [baseball] prospects."[76]

Tyson offers a sort of thesis statement on the matter. "You have to know struggle to be the champ," he says. The implication is that struggle makes you stronger. It makes you hungry, or forces you to apply yourself, or simply brings the best out of you. Highlighting struggle in athletes' stories also makes them seem more *deserving* of success, because they are no longer just lucky individuals blessed with physical "gifts." No one would look at Tyson's life as a poor juvenile delinquent in a rough neighborhood in Brooklyn and think, "That guy got all the breaks."

But struggle itself is not the special "something else" inside star athletes that makes them stars in these stories. It often forges or reveals meritorious traits and behaviors, but it isn't a crucial secret ingredient. Some athletes succeed without suffering much at all.

Hard work comes closer to being the "something else" that explains and justifies success. In addition to elevating Jordan, hard work is understood to make Bird special, closing the gap between him and those "lightning-quick black athletes." Katie Ledecky is described grinding: "The 4:05 a.m. wake-ups; the 20-minute predawn drives to the pool with one of her parents. . . . Day after day, year after year."[77] Many of the stars are said to have what you might call hard work–enabling traits. In Mattingly's case, it is "devotion" or "tenacity." For Ledecky it is "the absolute, burning desire to get better." For Trout it's drive. A profile of Williams cites "an obsessive attention to detail."[78]

Recall Michael Serazio's argument that sports "embeds a narrative that explains achievement in terms of meritocracy." That is, "winners succeed, sports tell us, because they work hard." By attributing success to hard work—the ingredient theoretically available to everyone—these stories imply that the meritocratic contest is fair and that athletes *deserve* their station. Sometimes the profiles state this outright. In naming Serena Williams 2015 Sportsperson of the Year, *Sports Illustrated* declared that her tennis victories were not sufficient reason for giving her the honor. "The trying is what's impressive. The trying is why we are here."[79]

But there are deviations from this formula. Hard work is not the only "something else" in these stories that sets star athletes apart. Savvy, for example, comes up numerous times: "'How do you differentiate the great athletes from the good ones?' asks [Bird's former teammate Dave] Cowens. . . . 'It's a savvy, or something. Larry's got it. Something mental that other players with more physical talent don't have.'"[80]

For tennis star Steffi Graf, psychological makeup and ability to perform in the clutch separate her from her competition.[81] Both Trout and Ledecky are described as being unafraid of failure. Williams's coach says: "There are very few champions on this planet, and they share things in common. . . . One of those things is the ability to forget the past. . . . They never look behind, always ahead."[82] Conor McGregor has "that thing that you can't teach people, whatever it is that makes people gravitate toward you."[83] Joyner-Kersee is "able to create the association between words and kinesthetic awareness right off the bat."[84]

The "something else" that makes athletes special is not always straightforward hard work: the trying is not the *only* reason we are here. And some of these other reasons, such as Graf's clutchness or Bird's savvy, are depicted as rare, elite capacities that require no more effort to develop than physical tools. They are "gifts." In fact, in some cases, hard work itself is portrayed as something of an innate ability. Mattingly's intensity, for example, "comes from within," according to the *New York Times*.[85]

This question of where the special something comes from— and who is responsible for it—is a preoccupation in these profiles. Several of the pieces ask which aspects of athletes' success are really under their control and which ones can be credited to the work or decisions of other people. The legendary trainer Cus D'Amato "made Mike [Tyson] from scratch," according to one quote in *Time* magazine.[86] Serena Williams was "groom[ed] for a takeover" by her father. "Outsiders often assume [Peter Graf] is the force behind [Steffi Graf's] career, a classic 'tennis parent,'" but this isn't correct. Graf "could have been born on the moon, and she still would be Steffi Graf."[87] Typically the profiles identify outside assistance in an athlete's life but conclude that the athletes' own abilities were the *real* differentiating factor in their success.

This idea of the athlete's "own" abilities can get muddy, however. "My mental game has always been from my dad," Serena Williams says in one *Self* magazine profile. The writer says in the next line that Williams's "physicality, however, is all her own."[88] The observation feels like a rejoinder—a defense of Williams against the accusation, made by Williams herself, that her father deserves some credit for her success. Never mind that Williams's parents could be said to have something to do with her physical skills. Here we have a writer crediting an athlete's physical gifts as the reason for her success because, hey, at least her father didn't give them to her. We've come full circle: in an attempt to show that an athlete's success is deserved, that success is attributed to her physical advantages.

I'm going to dig more into Americans' complex, sometimes contradictory ideas about agency in chapter 3, when I discuss my interviewees' thoughts on which of their positive qualities are their own. For now, I want to emphasize that American considerations of star athletes are shot through with uncertainty about deservedness. Even when you dominate multiple eras in your sport, win twenty-three grand slams, and are by near universal consensus one of the greatest athletes on earth, the role of *merit* in your success is a question in need of answering.

Idol Curiosity

If George H. W. Bush is asked why he should be at the top, if Hillary Clinton is accused of being the beneficiary of a rigged system, if Sheryl Sandberg says she succeeded in spite of, rather than because of, American institutions, and if journalists profiling LeBron James feel a need to explain that LeBron is more than just a winner of the genetic lottery, then American discourse about our "mass idols" is doing something other than telling us we live in a meritocracy.

Our discussions of these figures absolutely promote meritocracy. But they do so by advancing the premise that we should try to figure out whether the success of others is due to merit and celebrate them if it is. Having accepted these premises, we interrogate each individual idol's life, along the way wrestling with questions about rigged systems, unearned talent, and just plain luck.

If everyday Americans "collude" with these stories about our heroes in thinking about our own lives, as Karen Sternheimer argues, we likely do so by accepting the same premises, and then weaving narratives about ourselves that catalog the potential contributors to success and failure in order to take stock of whether we deserve what we have. What factors do we weigh? What standards do we use? I asked people.

2

Head Starts and Handicaps

Paul does not have a self-made story to tell, and he knows it. His father owns a successful business, and Paul was raised in comfort in a small town where he went to private school. When it came time for college, he studied hospitality, then took a front desk job at a hotel. "I was miserable doing it, obviously. Well, I shouldn't say miserable. It was a lot of work."

After a few years, he says, "my dad kind of needed me—not needed me, but kind of was ready to have me in the business if I wanted to be," Paul says. It wasn't a great fit. For starters, most of the guys in the company are "blue-collar, salt-of-the-earth" types, and he is not; many of them are mechanical, and he lacks that inclination. But he decided to do it anyway.

At first he was self-conscious about being "just the son." He wasn't fixing machinery, he wasn't making deals, he wasn't running the processing plant. Why was he there? But over time he found ways to make himself useful. Anything his father needed written, Paul wrote it. Any community issues that arose in the company's hometown, he dealt with them. He learned how to manage scheduling and operations. Now thirty-two, he feels respected and valued. He's a partner in the company, and comfortable.

He kinda-sorta likes his job. Paul gets a sense of pride from working with his family. More to the point, "I don't know what the hell I would be doing if I wasn't doing this," he says. "To live the lifestyle that I'm accustomed to, I couldn't afford it being a front desk manager."

I had a fair number of uncomfortable moments interviewing people about how they got to where they are in life and whether they deserved it. One man cried telling me he'd blown his inheritance on drugs. But I'm not sure there was any moment across sixty-plus hours of conversation when I felt more awkward than I did asking Paul whether circumstances had dictated his success, and to what extent he'd earned what he had. On the tape of our interview I can hear myself hem and haw as I round my way to the question. Paul took it in stride.

"I was clearly dealt a hand. . . . If I wasn't born into this, I would never be here," he began. "It's all circumstantial." But then he thought about it a little more. "The opportunity was there, but I took it," he said. "One thing my dad was good at was, he started me at the very bottom. . . . I worked my way up enough [to] where I don't feel like it was just handed to me. Like, blatantly handed to me." He decided that this was enough. "I think at this point I have earned the equity in the company that I now have."

I don't make the following point to criticize or disagree with Paul but to make a broader observation about American culture: *From a meritocratic standpoint,* the idea that Paul earned what he has is ridiculous. To reach the conclusion he does, Paul needs to use some other rationale, and a big part of his approach is to tell a story in which the external factors in his life are accounted for and explained. Such explanations are the subject of this chapter. We all experience variables outside our control in life; we all enjoy and endure advantages and disadvantages.

What do we tell ourselves and others about how those unearned advantages and disadvantages matter?

"And You May Ask Yourself, 'Well, How Did I Get Here?'"

If Americans were as naïve or credulous about meritocracy as we are sometimes made out to be, our answer to the question of how we got here, whether "here" is good or bad, should be something to the effect of "me." It is not, really.

The "principle of agency," as Robert L. Simon explains it, holds that "we deserve X (on grounds of merit) on the basis of Z only if Z is the result of the exercise of some quality of ours, and possession of that quality is not caused by factors beyond our control."[1] The American idea of merit, in other words, is at its crux a question of agency. I began all of my interviews by asking people to tell me where they are in life and how they got there. After they answered (which took some interviewees less than a minute and some close to an hour), I asked whether they felt successful, and to what they attributed their success or lack thereof. The stories people told to explain their standing in life virtually all involved multiple contributing factors, and by no means were all of those factors things they felt were under their control.

To some extent this is because agency is a difficult philosophical subject. You can get tangled up in fundamental matters of free will and the human condition. (Is God the true author of our fate? Do I deserve credit for my intelligence?) I'll discuss how people deal with some of these questions in chapter 3. But even at a more practical level, people were attuned to what I'll call "external" factors in their lives: structures and circumstances. We may think we deserve X on the basis of Z. But we know that A through M were involved too.

Consider these quotes:

- A thirty-seven-year-old woman who worked as a CFO said: "I was born into a situation where my parents could afford to send me to college. Could help me make good decisions about where I put my money. Could get me connections to talk to certain people about how to interview for jobs when I was 19 years old . . . . So I don't think that it's just, I decided that I was going to be successful and pull myself up by my bootstraps. I think I was set up in a way."
- A fifty-nine-year-old man who had been in and out of prison for much of his adulthood and never really held down a job said of his life: "It's the way the establishment is set up."
- Asked to what she attributed her success, a twenty-six-year-old medical student said: "My parents, definitely . . . . My dad taught us a lot about what you need to do to be successful in the world, especially as a black person, a black woman. And he gave us a really good example."

People understand that factors including parents and family, class, lucky breaks, help and hindrance from other people such as mentors and spouses, identity, and large political and economic forces—including, as we now know, global pandemics—all affect our trajectories profoundly. To say that Americans are aware of advantages, disadvantages, and other circumstances outside our control is not at all to say that we account for them *accurately*. But we do account for them, and typically feel a need to deal with them in our narratives, whether we conclude that we earned what we have or not.

Back in 1973, Richard Sennett and Jonathan Cobb noticed that working-class Americans were far from sold on the idea that American structures work the way they are supposed to. "Workingmen intellectually reject the idea that endless opportunity exists for the competent," they wrote.[2] Forty years later, Jennifer Silva found the same in interviews with working-class young adults, who saw (and bemoaned) the influence of economic structures in their own lives. But both also observed that their subjects still managed to conclude that they, personally, were in control of their own fate. "My biggest risk is myself," a thirty-four-year-old retail store manager told Silva.[3] The interviewees viewed external factors as *relevant* without treating them as *decisive*. This makes sense once you realize, as James Kluegel and Eliot Smith found, that Americans tend not to view individual and structural factors in their lives as alternatives—that is, more of one does not necessarily mean less of the other. Instead, they proposed, people tend to develop "compromise" views that incorporate both.[4]

How do such compromises get worked out? There's no single answer, of course. But this is where we can look for some insight to those "culturally coherent" storylines that people select off the cultural menu. There are many different subcultures in America with their own cultural stories, and myriad individual interpretations of them, some of which contradict one another. Still, time and again I found people using a few key narrative strategies to describe and assess the perceived advantages and disadvantages in their lives.

Silver Spoons and Striking Gold

There is a reason why riches-to-riches stories are not a beloved cultural trope. Americans know that there's less merit required to remain at the top than to rise to it. We have understood this for a long time—it's part of why Abraham Lincoln's presidential campaign emphasized his humble roots—but the idea has in recent years been discussed more and more in the cultural mainstream under the rhetorical umbrella of "privilege." Emerging from the jargony world of academia, the concept of privilege is now the subject of explainer quizzes on BuzzFeed and monologues from Tucker Carlson. The word means "unearned advantage,"[5] and its implications for meritocracy and merit are clear enough: it poses a challenge to them. Privilege can make the playing field uneven and invites questions about the extent to which *you* are responsible for your achievements.

Researchers studying privilege have found that individuals often resist acknowledging their unearned advantages.[6] This resistance is a function of "self-concern," write Eric Knowles and Brian Lowery. Regarding white people who deny white privilege, they argue, "Whites who endorse meritocracy seek to see themselves as personally possessing merit (i.e., talent and diligence), and deny the existence of racial inequities—specifically, unearned White privilege—that challenge this desired view of self."[7]

I did not find my interviewees to be shy about discussing advantages more broadly, however. Time and again, often without my prompting, interviewees included what they defined as advantageous situations in explanations of their lives. The more complicated and divisive questions in their stories were not *whether* many people enjoy advantages but which advantages matter and how much.

"A Well-to-Do Family": What Counts as an Advantage?

Darrell, a forty-two-year-old black man who blamed himself for having become an addict, described himself as coming from a "well-to-do" family. I imagined that his parents were doctors, lawyers, or businesspeople. Later on in the interview, Darrell elaborated: his mother had been a registered nurse and his father a truck driver. I don't mean to imply that such a family can't be comfortable, but it jumped out at me, perhaps because I was reading a lot of presidential candidates' campaign literature at the time, and politicians in this country have spun humble roots narratives out of much, much more. Since when does being a truck driver's son qualify as a head start?

Other interviewees described something more like what I'm used to thinking of as privileged socioeconomic roots: they had wealthy or upper-middle-class parents, and attended private or well-resourced public schools. Still others cited advantages that had nothing to do with money. People spoke of their parents' love or guidance, lucky breaks such as meeting a mentor at the right time, and enjoying good health as experiences that had given them a leg up in life. Pam, a thirty-four-year-old massage therapist, pointed to her appearance: "I'm a person that gets picked, I stand out in a crowd. And so often that's a good thing. . . . . I get chosen for the thing, or I get the job, or I got an A *even though*, or whatever it is. So I do have those experiences. I'm like a smiley girl with like big red hair. So I get attention without trying too hard."

A few interviewees even cited difficult experiences as advantages, explaining that struggle made them stronger. Hilliard, a biracial sixty-six-year-old, had grown up in a black neighborhood where he said he was often treated as an outsider. Kids picked on him and challenged him to fights, and it made him tough. "It's gotta be an advantage!" he said. "I'm here! I made it!"

I think of this last example as a different category of experience, because Hilliard is not discussing an *unearned* leg up; the process of surviving these experiences could very well be described as "earning." But the larger point is that advantage is a relative and subjective concept, and the range of experiences categorized as advantageous is broad.

Much of what Americans disagree about, when we debate our social and economic systems, is what constitutes an advantage. People of color often characterized whiteness as an advantage in American life, whereas white people didn't mention race in their accounts. It just wasn't a salient factor to them. This is consistent with work identifying whiteness as an "unmarked" case in American culture, which need not be considered the way race is for nonwhites, though survey research suggests that when you ask them, a majority of white people say that white people face discrimination in America.[8] So they are thinking about race a bit.

The closest my interviewees came to any kind of consensus on evaluating advantage is that *class matters*. You will sometimes hear analysts say that Americans don't think about class. In 2005, the *New York Times* began a big series on the subject by calling class "a dimension of the national experience that tends to go unexamined, if acknowledged at all."[9] With all due respect, I don't know what the *Times* was talking about. Americans discuss class *all the time*. My interviewees discussed the neighborhoods they grew up in, their parents' occupations, the quality of their schools, whether they had to pay their way through college, etc. They didn't agree about who is in what class. But class is broadly understood to reflect the opportunities available to an individual. In this sense, Americans are not describing in our stories a country that works purely meritocratically.

Even white people who believe themselves to be victims of discrimination are not telling a story in which Americans are on a level playing field. In fact, they are explicitly saying that we are not. They are just staking out a particular position on which way the incline tilts.

"Born on Second Base": Was Your Advantage Reasonable?

Mike, a white man who had grown up in a suburban area in a comfortable family and gone on to a happy and successful career in state government, used a helpful metaphor to characterize his background: he said he was "born on second base." Being born on third base is understood to be unattractive in American life, especially if you think you hit a triple, as Ann Richards famously said of George H. W. Bush. Being born on third means you don't have to do much to score. By contrast, being born on second is desirable but *reasonable*. You still have to run fast and hard, the thinking goes, to make it home.

When thinking about the relationship between advantage and the role of merit in their lives, one question people dealt with was how big an advantage was or is. A key strategy people used to address this question was to characterize their advantages as reasonable. Two common ways they did this were to describe an advantage as relatively common and/or an experience that everyone *should* have. Advantages characterized this way, I found, were treated as less of a threat to a person's ability to conclude he or she had earned success. This is why no interviewees who said they benefited from loving parents went on to say that this experience made them doubt their deservedness. Having good parents is understood to be relatively common, and in any case an experience to which everyone is entitled. It's an advantage, but people generally don't worry about its compromising their merit.

Similarly, Sara, a seventy-six-year-old half-Mexican woman, began our interview by offering a kind of thesis statement about her good fortune: "First off I would just like to say that, like a lot of people in this country, they're born here out of luck or circumstances. Some come to this country through their parents or grandparents, and that's how I got here, because if I had not been born here . . . . I would have been poor—poor-*er*—abject poverty. Also maybe one of those people that would have to be trying to cross the border and come over into the United States." Sara counted herself lucky in a global sense. But she was also confident that after a long career in city and state government, she had earned her secure retirement. Her luck had brought her reasonable opportunities on offer in America.

Many of my interviewees who believed they had benefited from socioeconomic comfort, quality education, good mentorship, and other fortuitous circumstances viewed themselves as participants in a meritocratic contest from which some (the rich) are excused and others (the poor) are excluded. They were in the reasonable middle, born on second base.

Does anything count as an *un*reasonable advantage? We characterize other people's advantages as unreasonable all the time. In telling our own stories, though, the main advantage that people describe as so consequential that it might cancel out the role of merit is a substantial socioeconomic edge. A small number of interviewees told me that their class privilege had been so vast that they weren't sure other factors in their lives mattered much at all. Laura, a twenty-seven-year old studying to be a therapist, said her father had a lot of money, which had given her time to flounder and find her way. She thought she might have been disadvantaged at times by being a woman, but "money outweighs and trumps so much else." She felt "shame" about her wealth, she said. Pam, the massage therapist, owned her own successful business. What separated her from her peers? "It's all about basically money," she said. Pam's parents had paid for her undergraduate education, which enabled her to graduate from school with less debt than her classmates. During her first couple of years in business, when she didn't make much money, she was able to live rent- and bill-free at her grandparents' house.

It's not a coincidence that both of these people are millennial women. Women in my interviews seemed generally more open than men to the possibility that they hadn't done things on their own, and millennials seemed more attuned to the role of privilege in their lives than their (our) elders. To actually conclude that one's advantages were so great that they were decisive in one's life was uncommon, however, across all demographics I interviewed. This is because we have some powerful storylines that help us avoid that conclusion.

"It's Not as If I've Just Coasted": Turning Advantage into Agency

The person who introduced me to Jon described him by saying he was going to be mayor someday. At twenty-eight, Jon was an alumnus of one prestigious university and was enrolled in a graduate program in another, and was well connected in Philadelphia's political community. I don't know if he'll be mayor, but it seemed to me that the guy was off to a good start. He thought so too: "I feel like the goals that I've set out to accomplish by this point in my life I have accomplished. I feel like they are maybe secondary or tertiary goals toward larger goals."

When I asked Jon to explain how he got where he is, he started his story with his family moving out of Philadelphia, into the suburbs, so he could attend the public schools there. The education he received, he said, had given him crucial reading, writing, and thinking skills. His parents then paid for his undergraduate education, and though he was footing the bill for grad school, he felt comfortable doing this because of the financial and emotional cushion his family provided.

He cited other advantages he had enjoyed. Jon was one of the few white people who mentioned race without any prompting from me. He said he thought being a white man had been a "big bonus" in terms of doors not being automatically closed to him. He also said, when I asked, that he did not consider himself to be especially naturally talented. "Most things that I think I'm good at I don't think are necessarily natural. I started learning how to write in Mr. Seymour's junior year class" in high school, he said.

And yet Jon did not attribute his success in life to luck. "To a large extent I don't believe in good luck," he said. Instead he believed in chance and preparation. He gave an example from his romantic life. Had he "lucked" into meeting his fiancée? Only if you ignored the effort he'd put in, he told me. "Is it lucky that I ended up having a lot of friends in common with my now fiancée and we ended up going to the same party? . . . . Yeah, it's lucky, but also I really tried to meet a lot of friends in town, and go out and be social."

Kluegel and Smith found that Americans need only believe in the existence of *some* opportunity to subscribe to individual explanations for achievement, and here we see one of the narrative justifications for that. By pursuing opportunity, many Americans believe, we contribute to our fortune. Sure, there's chance in life, but you can improve your chances. In this way, luck becomes at least in part a product of agency. Jon got some good opportunities. But he put himself in position to do so. He made his own luck, as the old saying goes.

Of course, not all luck can be explained this way. Jon's good education, his good family—he didn't create those advantages with hustle, and he was well aware of that. To explain this kind of edge, he used another common script, one I would argue is even more important to our narrative processing of advantage: you can *earn your luck retroactively.*

When I asked Jon if he felt he deserved his successes, he said yes, "because I feel like I've worked for them. Except for growing up in a nice household with parents who love me, and that support, I don't feel like anything else has been handed to me. . . . . Yes, I've certainly had a big leg up because of that privilege. Granted that I've had the leg up, it's not as if I've just coasted on that one leg up, you know. Every other step was me working my ass off to achieve what I want to achieve." He would feel differently about his advantages had he failed to make the most of them. "Had I got that leg up and then kinda coasted along . . . . just doing okay in school and enjoying growing up [in my neighborhood] and not really pushing myself or caring about things, then that would be in a way kind of unfair, unjust, what was given to me. But because I think I've pushed beyond that for things that are really difficult."

Time and again, asked about advantages and whether they had earned their success, interviewees said they felt they had because they used those advantages well. When I asked Laura, the twenty-seven-year-old studying to become a therapist who believed her father's money had "outweighed" so much else in her life, whether she deserved to be where she was, she said, "I would like to think that I do. I would like to think that despite the advantages that I had, I still work hard, I still am a compassionate person. I still hope to help others." In these behaviors she located her agency. Her origins were out of her control. "I can't change those things. I guess I could renounce—say, "Mom, Dad, don't ever help me, don't give me money, don't help me with anything." I don't know. I think asking for help, and having people that are able to help you, that's important." She seemed to be drifting toward an argument that her advantage is reasonable because people should have it.

It was noteworthy to me that several of the people with whom I spoke, like Laura, who said that their socioeconomic origins—their parents' money—had given them an enormous advantage emphasized *morality* as an important trait, and an important part of what gave them value as a person. They struggled to claim that they had earned their social positions, but they could find dignity elsewhere.

Awareness of privilege is a value of contemporary liberal politics. But while the conservatives I spoke with might have been less *concerned* about their unearned advantages, they acknowledged some, and used some of the same stories to explain good fortune in their lives. Gary, a fifty-seven-year-old Republican who owned and managed a retail store, had gotten some of the money to purchase the business from his father. He identified this as good fortune. But he felt that because he had put in a lot of work to make the business successful, and paid his father back, he had justified the opportunity.

"Dad put up guarantees . . . . he did back me, I think he lent me ten thousand dollars . . . . but he was paid back years ago—within a couple [of] years."

The flip side of this is that the few people I spoke with who said they had experienced advantages and been *un*successful, such as Darrell, the forty-two-year-old man who described his family as "well-to-do" and blamed himself for going on to become an addict, expressed not disappointment but *guilt* over having failed to control and capitalize on fortuitous circumstances. If one can earn one's advantages retroactively, these people felt in debt. They had failed to pay back their privilege.

Americans know that good luck can obscure the role of merit in an individual's life. But that doesn't mean we pretend it's not there, or conclude that success is arbitrary. Rather, we cite and assess advantages (with varying degrees of accuracy, and often using motivated reasoning) and then use a few common cultural stories to explain how we created or responded to them. We attempt to identify agency, take it out, dust it off, and take stock of the individual that way.

Humble Roots and Stumbling Blocks

Just as we address advantages in our stories, grappling with whether they explain success, we address disadvantages, grappling with a different set of questions: Can disadvantages be blamed for failures or shortcomings? Under what circumstances? And what do you say about your disadvantages if you succeeded in spite of them?

"I Didn't Grow Up in That"

What counts as a disadvantage in America today? The circumstances and experiences that interviewees characterized as unearned adversity, either implicitly or explicitly, included growing up poor in a bad neighborhood, suffering abuse and sexual assault, being orphaned at a young age, experiencing discrimination because of one's race or gender, disabilities, other health challenges for oneself or one's family, family discord, broad socioeconomic trends in one's industry, and coming from a comfortable middle-class, but not elite, background.

I do not mean to make fun of this last item. Scott, the man who mentioned it, regarded his background as a mild disadvantage and compared it to only some others'. He had grown up outside a midwestern city, the son of a librarian and a high school teacher. He said he had experienced advantages, too: being a man, being American, having parents who did a good job raising him. But after moving to the east coast, Scott had entered a social circle with people who came from more privileged backgrounds than he, and had come to view their advanced degrees and interesting careers as a result of an upbringing that he hadn't shared. Disadvantage, like advantage, is relative.

"I Can't Blame Nobody but Myself": *Disadvantage and Disappointment*

Thomas grew up "rugged," in a Philadelphia neighborhood dominated by gangs, without much attention from his mother ("she tried to have fun . . . she apologized to us later in life"), and got mixed up in the criminal justice system early, spending the latter portion of his youth in and out of juvenile detention. He resolved not to get arrested after he became a legal adult, but the plan didn't pan out. Shortly after his eighteenth birthday, Thomas told me, he was standing on a corner when a cop walked up to him and said, "Take your f——ing hand out your pockets." Then the cop hit him, he said. "And me being from the streets, the first thing I do is throw my hands up, because you ain't gonna hit me no more, now. . . . And he said, 'Are you throwing your hands up at me?'" The cop's partner hit Thomas, knocking him to the ground. "That kinda turned me out. . . . They gave me assault on a police officer, they sent me down. While I was in there, I just start think-ing, I'm always gonna get locked up no matter what." He began behaving accordingly. "There wasn't really nothing I could do about this situation, but what happened is, I allowed like a demonic spirit to lead me."

When I interviewed Thomas he was fifty-nine. He had spent much of his adult life incarcerated, to the point where, in looking back and telling his story, he spoke of prison as just another place he sometimes goes. In at least one instance, he says, he was locked up for a "racist ticket" he did not deserve, in others for infractions he admits he committed, and often for violating the terms of his probation. He had no job, no prospects, health problems, and bad relationships with many of his relatives, whom he considered bad influences. He was a nice guy.

Thomas recognized the powerful nature of the disadvantages he had experienced. "What you expect?" he said of his adult life, and observed that he has a brother who has been incarcerated for decades. The criminal justice system, he said, featured "a lot of injustice." But what was striking to me about Thomas, and other folks with whom I spoke who had spent time behind bars, is that they remained preoccupied with the nuances of their cases. They drew careful lines between their just and unjust arrests, and often ultimately held themselves accountable. "I made a lot of bad choices in my life," Thomas said, and "I can't blame nobody but myself a lot of the time." He even blamed himself for his failure to pay the racist ticket.

This was a common theme among interviewees disappointed in their working lives. They identified disadvantages they had suffered, but the bar for them to treat those disadvantages as decisive, and conclude that they *didn't* deserve their disappointments, appeared fairly high.

For starters, people seemed to feel compelled to make a case that their disadvantages were unreasonable, and not outweighed by good fortune they had enjoyed, if they were to conclude that those advantages mattered a lot. Susan, a middle-aged office manager who didn't think much of what she had accomplished, had grown up in wealth and comfort, then married a man who subsequently left her to raise their child on her own. She moved to Philadelphia, took a "completely random" job because it provided health insurance for her son, and never got a career related to her interests off the ground. I thought being left by her husband to raise a child sounded like a pretty big setback, and I said so. But Susan did not see things that way. "Lots of people do that—raise a kid and have a job and do it all," she said. She viewed the class privilege of her upbringing as far more important than her husband ditching her, and blamed herself for failing to take advantage of it.

Even people who described their disadvantages as substantial could conclude that the influence of their circumstances was outweighed by their mistakes. Darrell had struggled with discrimination throughout his youth. Growing up, he said, "I was always labeled as effeminate, I was labeled as gay. I didn't know how to throw a ball like a boy. I didn't know how to kick a ball like a boy. And therefore I experienced a lot of ridicule growing up in school. That impacted my self-esteem greatly." As an adult, he identified as a gay man but struggled to reconcile this identity with his Christian background. He described these experiences as disadvantages, and meaningful ones. But he did not consider them sufficient to remove the blame for his failures from his own shoulders. "I think life has been fair. But I think I haven't been fair to myself," he said. He regretted that he allowed "peer pressure" to influence him. "I feel as though I earned where I am. And it's crippling."

Like Thomas, Darrell looked at his life, saw clear and substantial disadvantages that were way out of his control . . . . and then asked whether he had nevertheless made *significant enough mistakes* to justify taking the onus of his disappointments onto himself. He decided that, yes, he had. This was a common approach to explaining disadvantage.

It wasn't universal. In the introduction I wrote about Philip Mitchell, the twenty-five-year-old college graduate who worked stocking shelves, was frustrated by this situation, and did not feel it was his fault. He said he had done everything he was supposed to do, and the country wasn't delivering on its promises. Similarly, Linda ran a dairy farm for decades with her husband. Their professional and economic lives, she said, had suffered because of a global disregard for farmers.

"All across the world, farmers are not treated well, not paid well," she said. She looked at what milk cost, and how much of that money made it back to the farm. "Someone is getting two hundred and eleven dollars," per hundred pounds, she said, and she and her husband would receive sixteen dollars, maybe twenty. She pointed to truck drivers, advertisers, and brokers as middlemen who jump in between the farmer and the customer and grab hold of the money, taking advantage of the fact that the farmer has to sell cheap and fast because "the product we produce is extremely perishable." She said she had earned more than the American economy had paid her.

Large economic forces like the ones Philip and Linda said set them back can be viewed as extremely powerful influences on our lives. Other kinds of disadvantages can too, including injury, illness, and the malice or incompetence of others. People like Linda and Philip, who cited a substantial disadvantage *and* felt comfortable saying they had not made important mistakes that explained their disappointments, could construct a story in which they deserved better than they got.

It's too early, as I write this, to say very much about how COVID-19 fits into this picture. But assuming we experience massive economic disruption, as seems quite possible, I expect more Americans will begin to tell stories in which their economic fate was out of their own control, because their businesses closed, industries collapsed, etc. Others who suffer will look around and notice that *some* people were not laid off or professionally derailed, and conclude that because such a trajectory was possible, they should be held accountable for their failure to achieve it. Still others will struggle and survive or even thrive—which brings us to another important storyline.

"I Had to Do It": Disadvantage and Success

The classic American story about disadvantages in a person's life, of course, involves the individual overcoming them. It's Horatio Alger: using your wits and working hard, you rise up from humble roots, overcome obstacles, and become great.

Among my interviewees, however, many people who felt successful said they had struggled with obstacles, made some progress, and became just *good*. Their disadvantages don't stop them in their stories but do hold them back somewhat. People say they would have gone further or made more money had it not been for limited opportunities, discrimination, the logistical trouble of a health issue, etc.

"There are institutions, there are laws, there are attitudes . . . that are designed to keep black people, women, and other minorities down," said June, a sixty-one-year-old black woman. June had attended a prestigious university but dropped out because she couldn't afford it. She started and stopped college several times before eventually collecting her degree. Finally, slowly, she built a career, first selling ads and then teaching continuing education courses.

June felt successful and satisfied. But it was clear to her that with as much intelligence and drive as she had, she would have gone further on a level playing field. She could have finished college more quickly, launched her career sooner, and experienced more success. Even now, she says, the men who do the same job that she does get paid more for poorer work.

The idea of origins or obstacles circumscribing opportunities and limiting success is extremely common. It comes up most frequently in the context of class and community background. When I asked Kia, a thirty-four-year-old social worker, whether she felt successful, she said, "Have I beat some of the odds? Yes. I came from North Philly, where it was guns, drugs around me every day. I'm no longer in that environment." But, she told me, "I'm still a female, I'm still black, and I'm still Muslim. I have three odds against me. I don't make as much as you." Others noted disadvantages such as mental health struggles or traumatic experiences holding them back and said they had done well, considering.

For those who said they had overcome obstacles completely, a common theme was to describe their disadvantages as sort of *stealth advantages*. Carl, the sixty-nine-year-old owner of a contracting company, had grown up dirt poor, raised by his sharecropper grandparents, eating ketchup-and-mustard sandwiches. His first job out of the service was a "nasty, nasty" one cleaning oil burners. These experiences, he argued, forced him to develop the work ethic that had been key to his success. "I didn't have anything," he said, so he learned to try. Likewise, a twenty-six-year-old medical student thought her father's death "pushed me forward." What didn't kill them made them stronger.

It's important to note, though, that somewhere in the process of turning a disadvantage into an advantage, agency kicks in. Carl says he had to do it—but at the end of the day, *he did it*, and the fact that he did means that other people who grew up the way he did could or should have done the same thing. The difficulty of disadvantage is narrated away by the opportunity to emerge from it stronger and better.

"What doesn't kill you makes you stronger" is, of course, a popular and inspiring notion in American culture. It is also an example of external factors in a person's life being recognized, considered, and then subordinated to individual agency. Life isn't fair, but if the unfairness throws you off, that's usually on you.

Sticking to the Scripts

Paul says he has earned the equity he has in his father's company "at this point." This means at some prior point he had not. Earlier in his career, he concedes, external factors brought him undeserved rewards. Somewhere in between then and the time when we spoke, he said, he had done *enough* on his own to warrant his position. He tipped the scale sufficiently in favor of agency and awarded himself the dignity of deservedness.

Undoubtedly someone reading this disagrees with Paul's conclusion. The meaning of "enough" depends on all kinds of subjectivities, motivations, and judgment calls, including where you're from, to whom you compare yourself, and whether you *want* to conclude that you earned what you have—considerations I'll discuss in chapter 4. But a key step of the assessment is taking stock of advantages and disadvantages and explaining their role in your life. The answer to the mystery of how Paul concludes he's earned it is that he's able to construct a culturally coherent story that deals adequately with his head start.

Our culture provides us with storylines that help with this. Paul uses a storyline about earning his advantages retroactively;

Thomas uses one about making important mistakes; many of us say we were born on second base. These storylines are the "good reasons" of narrative rationality, the justifications that make sense to Americans. Most but not all of them nudge us toward the conclusion that we do in fact get what we deserve. They are the stories of an individualistic culture. But they're flexible.

I want to be clear again that I'm not saying Paul, Thomas, Jon, Pam, or anyone else is being unethical or unreasonable in how they talk about their advantages and disadvantages. But what they're not being is meritocratic. From a meritocratic standpoint, the idea that you can earn advantages retroactively doesn't make sense. If you and I compete for the same job, and I get the job because my father is the boss, the fact that I subsequently work hard and do well doesn't make my success meritocratic. Likewise, if you make one medium-sized mistake in the interview process, it doesn't change the fact that you were at a significant disadvantage from the get-go.

What we attempt to do in our stories is to *account for* and *explain* advantages and disadvantages so that we can focus on the things we control and take stock of individual merit. It's a fraught, complicated process. And there's another wrinkle: our notion of which qualities and behaviors in our lives are actually under our control—and which of them make us deserving of reward—is much less than clear-cut.

3

Me, Myself, and I

If you inherit a million bucks from your parents, it's clear enough that you didn't earn the money. But there are more ambiguous cases. Remember that Americans have expressed doubts about whether a star athlete like Shaquille O'Neal earned his success (he's tall and strong, but did he *do* anything?) and whether a politician like Jesse Jackson earned his prominence (he got a lot of attention, but did he do anything *good*?). These kinds of questions, about what exactly we deserve credit for, can fairly be asked about any of us. Does a seventeen-year-old with a knack for test-taking deserve the fruits of a high SAT score? Does an ambitious person who aggressively sells himself to his bosses deserve that promotion more than his quiet, humble coworker? Does a man deserve blame for his lack of zeal if that deficit—if *who he is*—is the result of the way he was raised?

This last question came up in the interview I did with Kia, the thirty-four-year-old social worker, whom I met in a community center while she waited for her kid to finish swim class. Kia wore a burqa. She told me about her childhood in a rough Philly neighborhood, where "it was guns, drugs around me every day," and how she found her way out by studying hard, going to an SAT prep program on Saturday mornings rather than sleeping in, and getting a scholarship to college. Her older brother did not do these things, and at the time we spoke, he was in prison. Kia said her brother was smart but lacked motivation and "zeal." She attributed these shortcomings in large part to his upbringing. Whereas Kia had been required to help with laundry, cooking, and caring for their younger siblings, as a male her brother had been allowed to coast. "All his life everything has been given to him," she said, echoing Eric Mitchell's take on his brother Philip. "He doesn't want to do, because I feel like he doesn't have to do." Even now, she said, "people are still enabling him."

It seemed to me that Kia was laying most of the blame for her brother's situation at their family's feet. If this was their fault, I asked, did her brother deserve the consequences? Was he in prison because of *him*?

She answered me, and I'll discuss how in a bit, because her answer was interesting. But I want to note first how she seemed to feel about the question. She seemed annoyed.

Neither philosophers nor psychologists nor theologians have offered a definitive account of human agency and free will, and they probably won't. Neither will I in this chapter. I also won't tell you definitively whether someone like Kia's brother deserves what he got by American standards, because there is no single American standard for what it means to deserve something. Rather, I want to explore the individual traits and behaviors Americans highlight when we talk about how we got to where we are, consider which of those we say are under our control and which make us deserving of reward. Put another way, I want to see what specific qualities play the part of merit in our stories.

I think I annoyed Kia for two reasons. First, I probably seemed like yet another person making excuses for her brother, who she already felt was let off the hook too much. Second, my line of questioning was inherently annoying. It probably seemed *designed* to produce an answer that was in some way confused or arbitrary, because Kia didn't have a lot of good answers available to her. The explanations on offer in American culture for when and why we become responsible for our socioeconomic situations, whether raking in a fortune or sitting in a prison cell, are deeply disputed and pretty vague.

After listening to my interviewees grapple with the roles of potentially meritorious factors like talent, hard work, drive, grit, decision making, morality, and frugality in their lives, the closest I can come to a unifying explanation of merit is this: we exercise our agency by making *choices*, and we pay for deservedness with our most fundamental resources, our *time* and our *comfort*. Behaving morally is a necessary but insufficient condition. So, for instance, Shaq didn't make a choice to be big. He made a choice to use that quality, which makes him deserving of some reward—though he would be more deserving if he had sacrificed more time and comfort in his pursuit. He could enhance or compromise his deservedness with moral or immoral behavior.

There are exceptions and contradictions even within this admittedly broad framework. And significantly, this definition of merit, which we use when discussing the deservedness of individuals, is not the same version of merit that meritocratic systems seek to reward, even in theory. Choosing to sacrifice time and comfort is not necessarily how you show a company you are the right person for the job or gain admission to Harvard.

In describing the difference between what she called "official" and "unofficial" heroes, Joan Didion wrote of "the apparently bottomless gulf between what we say we want and what we do want, between what we officially admire and secretly desire, between, in the largest sense, the people we marry and the people we love."[1]

There is some of this dynamic at play in the American construction of merit: a distance between the qualities we explicitly say deserve reward and the qualities we actually promote and celebrate. In this chapter I take a close look at what Americans say is meritorious in our stories—the qualities we marry. Later I'll suggest that we would do well to stick with our spouse.

Loosely Defined

If you grow up in New York City, and your parents can't afford to send you to an expensive private high school, it has generally been understood that your best chance at a high-caliber education that makes you a competitive applicant to a prestigious college is to gain admission to one of the city's eight selective public high schools.

At this writing, admission to these schools is based on students' scores on a single test, known as the Specialized High School Admissions Test (SHSAT), which students take in eighth or ninth grade. In recent years, however, this system has come under fire, as black and Hispanic admissions to the specialized high schools plummeted to an embarrassing level: 70 percent of all public school students in New York City are black and Hispanic, but only 10 percent of specialized school students. In 2019 only *seven* of 895 students admitted to Stuyvesant High School, the system's flagship institution, were black.[2]

Media coverage and political conversation have focused on the proliferation of test prep programs as a driving factor behind the disparity. And so, after the 2019 admissions statistics were released, New York City mayor Bill de Blasio presented a plan to scrap the SHSAT entirely and replace it with a system that would award seats to top-performing students from every middle school in the city.

He framed this first and foremost as an attempt to achieve greater fairness in selecting qualified students. "If we want this to be the fairest big city in America, we need to scrap the SHSAT and start over," he wrote in an op-ed.[3]

It should be noted, though, that the mayor was also proposing to change the *definition* of a qualified student. The kid who gets good grades in middle school and the kid who aces an entrance exam are not necessarily the same kid, even absent considerations of test prep programs. Getting good grades and performing well on a single test certainly don't require the same efforts and abilities. In asking New York to reconsider admissions criteria, de Blasio was asking New York to reconsider the meaning of merit.

This is a long-standing tradition in American education.[4] Once upon a time the Harvard entrance exam was based on the curricula of old money New England feeder schools, and the men who attended such schools were the ones who gained admission to Harvard. In the middle of the twentieth century, a Harvard president named James Bryant Conant began to believe that the nation's elite was becoming calcified, and in an effort to find and promote an "aristocracy of talent," he advocated for the adoption of the Scholastic Aptitude Test as an admissions criterion for American colleges. It caught on. (There's a fascinating account of Conant's project in *The Big Test* by Nicholas Lemann.)[5] Essentially, Conant redefined merit as intelligence reflected by performance on the SAT. Incoming classes indeed began to look different, and not always in ways that pleased administrators. There were more Jews, more African Americans, more graduates of public high schools. Fearing that Harvard would admit "an army of future Ph.D.s" who would be "pansies and poets and serious la-de-da types," the school introduced new indices of merit again, including athletic and extracurricular achievement.[6]

Institutions often come under fire for manipulating the measure of merit to suit their purposes, whether improving diversity, keeping out the "la-de-da" types, or whatever else. Critics suggest that the tail is wagging the dog, and deservedness is being determined before it is measured. But redefining merit isn't necessarily cynical. Merit can be defined in more or less successful ways, and it often makes sense to adjust an institution's approach. What it cannot be is defined *absolutely*. In fact, the reason why institutions are forever debating merit criteria is that the meaning of merit is fluid, context-dependent, and ultimately in the eye of the beholder.

Defining merit in the context of admission to educational institutions has always been a complex endeavor because of the various concerns at play: Is Stuyvesant High School trying to reward the students who have studied hardest? Who *will* study hardest? Who are most adept with numbers? Who *could be* most adept with numbers? But education, as a sector of American life that Americans have long associated with the promise of meritocracy, is actually an area in which these concerns are relatively carefully thought out. Things get even more complicated when we zoom out to the context of American society and consider what merit means in relation to socioeconomic rewards generally (i.e., money and status).

A "functional" definition of merit in this context, writes Richard Longoria, begins with the question "How well can we expect this person to do the job at hand?" He goes on, "Innate talent and the propensity to make an honest effort are likely to figure highly in this regard. [This approach] then rewards the person who we expect to perform well."[7]

But "can you do the job?" isn't the whole story, not least because we often assess merit not in a predictive context but in a reflective one. We ask not just whether Donald Trump will do a good job as president but what all the factors were that went into his becoming rich and famous in the first place. As I noted in the introduction, Stephen McNamee and Robert Miller argue that merit in America today consists of some combination of innate talents and abilities, attitude, hard work, and moral character.[8] This strikes me as a good starting point. But merit evolves. Witness the excitement not long ago over the notion of "grit." When Angela Duckworth introduced the idea that "perseverance and passion for long term goals" were a better predictor of individual success than talent, she was throwing a monkey wrench into our contemporary concept of merit.[9] And people liked it.

What's more, merit is perhaps more philosophically complicated than this definition allows. Fundamentally, merit is about what is deserved, and one might argue, as Jonathan Mijs does, that talent "is not meritocratically deserved."[10] It might be conceived as random luck or an unearned inheritance. And while we might first associate talent with qualities like intelligence, athletic ability, or a nice singing voice, who's to say that the very ability to work hard isn't a genetic predisposition? None other than conservative hero Milton Friedman posited that the qualities of being hardworking and thrifty "owe much to the genes [a man] was fortunate (or unfortunate?) enough to inherit."[11]

No "effort gene" has actually been found . . . yet, as Longoria notes. But let's posit that hard work isn't genetic—let's say it's "nurture" rather than "nature." John Rawls argued that "the willingness to make an effort, to try, and so to be deserving in the ordinary sense is itself dependent on . . . social circumstance." If so, it's still not clear the quality would be deserved: "The assertion that a man deserves the superior character that enables him to make the effort to cultivate his abilities is especially problematic: for his character depends in large part upon fortunate family and social circumstances for which he can claim no credit."[12] Down this philosophical path lies considerable logistical trouble. "If everything is arbitrary a person could no longer be held accountable for their actions because their choices and efforts are considered to be beyond their control," writes Longoria. "Criminals could not be justifiably penalized because their actions were a result of their environment, not individual volition. Athletes could not deserve trophies because someone else, like parents or coaches, determined the effort the athlete expended at training. And employees could not request a salary in exchange for choosing to work, since they aren't responsible for wanting to be productive and make an effort."[13]

Fair enough. But the point still stands that these are open philosophical issues. When it comes to what we control and what we deserve as a result, we are all invited to be philosophers and construct stories and explain our lives in ways that reflect our own understanding of what merit means. What I want to consider in this chapter is our treatment of individual traits and behaviors in these stories, which I divide into four very broad categories: innate abilities, effort, decisions, and morals. I'll discuss what roles we say they play in our success or failure, and whether and when we say these qualities deserve reward.

America's Got Talent (but Not Too Much of It): Innate Abilities

"How smart are you?" I asked Doug, sitting in his mansion.

Doug, fifty, was in his glorious home outside Philadelphia speaking to me in the middle of the day because, having made a substantial amount of money in both research and real estate, he now does what he wants. He is involved in angel investing and mentoring, which he finds "hugely" and "cosmically" rewarding. For kicks, he helps open businesses in underserved communities.

I found myself asking questions like "How smart are you?" directly because my interviewees rarely brought up innate strengths or weaknesses on their own when I asked them to tell me how they got to where they are. Whether this was honest or false humility I cannot say. But people didn't often foreground talent in their success or failure stories.

For his part, Doug replied that he was "smarter than average." He told me he had the highest SAT score in his graduating class, won national science fairs in his youth, and just naturally has an inclination toward figuring out how things work. But he emphasized that smarts didn't get him where he was. He mentioned a girl he knew growing up who was the smartest of the smart kids, but struggled because of other issues. Plenty of people in his PhD cohort were smarter than he but didn't complete the degree, he said.

This kind of wishy-washy assessment of talent and its role in life was typical. When I asked about their talents, interviewees described themselves as "mechanically inclined," "adept with numbers," naturally good with people, a "quick study," and generally intelligent. A dancer said he had an innate understanding of how his body works. (No one got philosophical and expressed uncertainty about which qualities are innate.) Interviewees who responded to my questions about talent by *rating* their talents tended to place themselves somewhere in the middle of the bell curve. Not one interviewee said his or her talents were exceptional, and few described themselves as substantially lacking in natural ability. A man named Hassan who immigrated from the Middle East to get a graduate degree, then rose to the top of his industry before launching his own multimillion-dollar company, had a strikingly roundabout way of saying he was pretty smart: "there is enough evidence" that his family is "above average in terms of smarts . . . and social skills, and basic talent," he said. He noted that both he and his brother were pretty good at math in school.

I certainly don't mean to suggest that Americans are categorically opposed to bragging about talent. The man who received 63 million votes in the 2016 presidential election once tweeted, "Sorry losers and haters, but my I.Q. is one of the highest—and you all know it!" But on balance, my interviewees said that talent had been *helpful* in their lives rather than *decisive*. "Your talent can only take you so far," explained Erica, a twenty-four-year-old woman studying to be an EMT. Susan, the middle-aged office manager who regarded her career as a disappointment, blamed her decision making and work ethic, and said her talent had only enabled her to avoid doing worse. "I am smart, and that made things easier throughout life," she said. In our stories, talent is framed as a predisposition that could be made useful with effort or squandered without.

What Talent Deserves

Why one person is smart, another is good with numbers, and a third jumps high is a matter of some dispute in American culture. Among my interviewees, some said they viewed talent in religious terms, as a gift from God that the individual is free to use (or not) as he or she sees fit. But whether religious or not, interviewees tended to characterize talent as something outside of individual control, and thus not really at the crux of what it means to earn something.

Hassan, for example, initially told me he was "the definition of meritocracy," but as our interview progressed, it became clear he was well aware of the influence of structural, circumstantial, and coincidental factors in his life. I wondered what, exactly, he thought made his case so meritocratic.

"Your contribution to life is relative," he explained. "You have certain assets. Those assets sometimes you are born with, and sometimes you actually enhance through life. . . . Your name, your looks, your height, your smarts, all of that you had nothing to do [with]. . . . The question really in my opinion is, your contribution then to society has to be driven by the relative assets that you started with." You *earn* something by "taking the assets that you have and leveraging them."

Hassan seemed to put his smarts in the same category as one might put Shaq's size—or someone's family connections, for that matter. I heard this characterization of talent from others as well. Philip Mitchell (the twenty-five-year-old whose older brother put him "on blast" in the introduction) was an aspiring actor in addition to working toward a career in communications. But whereas Philip felt he deserved a job in communications, he did not feel he deserved acting gigs—even though he considered himself a talented actor. His talent did not make him deserving. You have to take initiative with your talent to deserve reward.

This raises the somewhat vexing question of whether the perceived *absence* of talent can make someone undeserving. If you pursue something but don't have the natural ability to make it happen, do you deserve to fail?

Anita is a thirty-seven-year-old woman who had bounced from a job at a box store to one at a big delivery company to one working as a waitress to a job in a hotel kitchen. She told me very frankly that she did not have a high estimation of her own abilities. "I don't feel like I really got too much to offer" in the working sphere, she said. Years ago Anita wanted to be a court stenographer, but things didn't work out. She blamed herself—but not for lacking talent. "I didn't do what I was supposed to do to make it better. . . . I could've went back to school. I didn't," she said.

There is a blurry line, I noticed doing these interviews, between what Longoria calls "abilities," which "can be gained through proper training," and "capabilities," which are innate and distributed at birth.[14] You can see why. Is the child of musicians, raised in a home filled with music and given many opportunities and much encouragement to play, demonstrating talent or development when she turns out to be a great musician in her own right? Ambiguity is a reasonable state for these concepts.

One implication of this ambiguity is that narrative accountability becomes flexible. Anita, who seemed inclined to want to beat herself up, chose to blame her disappointment on her failure to acquire abilities rather than her lack of capability to do so. This is a simple narrative to tell if the upshot of your story is that you deserve a bad outcome. People who didn't tell that kind of story, but still needed to explain disappointment, were more likely to say that they were just "not cut out" for something, without the negative judgment. They lacked the necessary talent—not their fault.

Lacking talent doesn't mean you deserve to *succeed* at something. It's just not the best reason to offer for why you deserved to fail. It is possible to imagine someone saying she deserves failure because she wasn't smart enough, fast enough, mechanically inclined enough, etc. But this premise comes up less often in our stories than the idea that deservedness is related to the actions we took to develop and use our talents. We regard innate talent as too secondary, too pliable, and ultimately too far outside the individual's control to link it directly to what we deserve.

The downplaying of talent in our stories is not consistent with how talent is treated in other aspects of American culture. In some contexts we celebrate natural "gifts" quite a lot. I'll discuss this discrepancy later in this chapter. But in my interviews, the reluctance to foreground talent was strong.

One twenty-one-year-old named Chris, a recent graduate of community college with plans to go into education, went so far as to say that if you acquire something because of innate talent, you won't keep it. He told me a story to illustrate the point. Chris's father was always complaining about his phone, he said. Chris had a newer, nicer phone than his dad. So, Chris told me, "I let him borrow my phone for a week and I switched it, I took his phone for a week." When they checked in, Chris discovered that "[my dad] having a better phone didn't erase any of the problems that he was having." The problem wasn't what his father had. It was what he did with it.

"Natural ingenuity is only going to go so far," Chris said. "If you haven't earned it, you'll lose it." As for how to earn it, he said, "If you work at something . . ."

Work It: Effort

I had a confusing conversation with Ronald, a forty-six-year-old handyman who had grown up in a tough neighborhood and, though he had never really gotten a consistent career off the ground, felt relatively successful compared to the men he'd grown up around, many of whom wound up in the drug trade. When I asked him what he thought separated people who succeed from those who don't, he said, "Hard work, hard work," and "Good things come to those who work." Then he went on.

> *Ronald:* Laziness don't get you nothing. But drug dealers not lazy, there's hard work in that too. You gotta worry about the police, then you gotta worry about competition. Then you gotta worry about your product you selling. So that's work too.
>
> *Doron:* So then the difference isn't hard work? Because the drug dealers are working hard too?
>
> *Ronald:* They're working hard.

Ronald says that hard work is what makes people successful, and drug dealers aren't successful. Then he says that drug dealers work hard.

Sadly for me, an awkward pause followed and I didn't dig into this. But here is the push-and-pull over the role of hard work in American life. We *want* hard work to be the key to success, but we're not sure how often it is, and we may not be entirely clear what we mean by it.

The notion of "hard work" occupies a hallowed position in the American mind. John Gardner, writing in 1961, observed that in Britain, when a child doesn't know an answer in school, he is told, "You are not up to this." In America he's told, "You need to study harder."[15] Hard work has been a virtue in American culture from the nation's earliest days, when the Protestant work ethic was embraced by settlers as a form of service to God. This tenet paved the way for the idea that people should work for advancement, and work is of course very much still accepted as laudable behavior.

While my interviewees seemed reluctant to foreground talent in explanations of how they got to where they are, many seemed perfectly comfortable proclaiming how hard they worked, from a road crew worker ("Whatever job you do, whether it's cleaning toilets or whatever, whether you like it or not, just do the best job you can") to a wealthy financial consultant ("How did you get here?" "Hard work"). Hard work was understood to activate other factors, such as luck or talent. Paul's getting a job with his father wouldn't matter unless he worked hard, and Doug's intelligence wouldn't have taken him very far if not accompanied by effort. Along the same lines, the absence of hard work could be understood to be decisive in a way that the absence of talent was not. Susan, the office manager, attributed her failure to rise to her "laziness." A forty-four-year-old man named Mark who was frustrated to be stocking shelves at a grocery store explained, "I haven't put all the effort in that I could."

Yet there was no consensus that hard work always or even usually *works*. Linda, the retired dairy farmer, could hardly have imagined working harder but did not feel that her efforts had paid off. "The old adage that if you worked harder you'd get more money does not hold true in farming," she said (working smarter, she said, maybe). Curtis, a forty-nine-year-old who had bounced from job to job and was fighting for Social Security disability insurance, said he had worked hard and not reaped the benefits. There was also a substantial number of interviewees who said that, though hard work had paid off for them personally, there were lots of *other* people for whom it hadn't.

Americans are divided, then, on the question of whether hard work reliably helps you in life. But we are rather unified on the question of whether it should. Time and again, people who felt successful pointed to hard work as the reason why their success was warranted. The connection seemed obvious to them. "All I can say is that I've worked really hard," said Diana, a twenty-six-year-old woman who had recently completed a degree, when I asked whether she had earned it. Connie, a seventy-seven-year-old retired educator, in response to a similar question, said, "Oh, who deserves anything?" and then decided that yes, she probably deserved what she had, because she had worked very hard. "I've earned it. Part of it was earned. I earned it. I worked hard," said Leonard, a fifty-two-year-old catering manager. "Earning" in particular seemed to be associated with hard work, but deserving was as well.

Along the same lines, several people who felt unsuccessful and didn't think they deserved better said this was because they had not worked hard enough. And people who thought they deserved better than they got tended to highlight the fact that they had worked hard but not been rewarded. In short, most people drew a straight line from hard work to socioeconomic deservedness. Working hard is viewed as being unambiguously under one's own control, a resource available to more or less everyone, and so deserving of reward in a meritocracy.

Note, though, that "hard work" is not the only imaginable explanation for how a person could earn or deserve something. Asked whether they earned their success, someone might coherently say, "I completed the tasks I was assigned," or "I outperformed the competition," or "I treated people well along the way." Our focus on hard work as a justification for reward is not definitional but a choice many of us make about how to talk about deservedness in our lives.

Some interviewees elevated hard work to the level of a moral principle, calling it the right thing to do regardless of what it might do for them. Joe, a twenty-eight-year-old assistant manager at a retail store, had gone to college and studied to be a draftsman, then worked as one until the home-building industry collapsed. He had lost faith in the American economic system and had no expectation that it would reward him appropriately. But he intended to work hard in any case. "I don't know if I subscribe to the idea of an appropriate place. I believe a lot in hard work," he said. People who were said not to have worked hard were sometimes described as having done something wrong.

What Is Hard Work?

Among the people who told me they worked hard were a dairy farmer, a graduate student, a financial consultant, a fireman, an assistant manager at a retail store, a housewife, and a corporate lawyer. One thing you might notice about these people is that their work lives probably don't have a lot in common. I began to wonder what people meant by hard work.

I didn't expect there to be a single, concrete answer (like "milking cows") because, among other problems, what's difficult for me is not necessarily difficult for you. Still, there could be some patterns in how hard work registered in people's lives, or what it required of them. So I took a look at what people talked about when they talked about hard work, and in some cases asked them what they meant specifically.

For a number of interviewees, it was clear that part of working hard was the amount of time spent working. They talked about holding down multiple jobs or pulling sixty-hour work weeks. "I worked all the time," said Carl the contractor. His daughter, he said, would cry if her mother wasn't around because she didn't know who he was. "That's how many hours I worked."

"Getting up at five thirty or six o'clock in the morning every day, not wasting time," said Jeff, a forty-year-old businessman, when I asked what hard work meant to him. But then he elaborated. "Just being in an office isn't hard work." There was more to it, he said.

Joe, the retail store assistant manager who viewed hard work as a moral imperative, also said that time wasn't necessarily the crux of the issue. "Whether you work forty hours or forty-eight hours, it doesn't matter," he said. He found value in "going the extra mile" for a customer, sometimes double- or triple-checking his work. For him, hard work meant insisting on doing things well.

Still others emphasized the "hard" part of hard work, indicating that real hard work involved suffering or struggle. Philip Mitchell told me that he worked hard because he was on his feet all day. Susan admired her husband's work ethic, saying that he doesn't sleep because of stress. Eric Mitchell said he had worked, because he put in time, but wasn't sure he had worked *hard*, because many things had come easily to him.

One of the things Anita said she had earned in life was the longevity of her marriage and providing her children with a two-parent household, something she had accomplished, she said, by putting work into it. This meant looking beyond herself, "[putting up with] infidelity, stuff like that." For her and for others, hard work meant a combination of putting one's time into something, trying to do it well, and sacrificing to make it so.

Notice the fluidity of this idea. You can call yourself a hard worker if you play golf every day after putting painstaking effort into three dental surgeries, and you can be lazy if you stock shelves at Target for forty hours per week without pursuing advancement. At the same time, you can be lazy if you play golf every day after putting painstaking effort into three dental surgeries and a hard worker if you stock shelves at Target for forty hours per week without pursuing advancement.

Hard Work's Cousins: Drive and Grit

Wilson, a fifty-seven-year-old veteran, had been a graphic illustrator in the service—a desirable position for him that was not easy to come by, particularly, he thought, for a black man. He landed the job by working hard, but in a very specific way that warrants attention. He hustled. He got out and found the right people to talk to, got on their radar, and sold himself.

Here, hard work overlaps with drive, or ambition. Drive usually involves hard work, but it is not the same thing. Drive is the application of work directed toward a specific goal—not just showing up and trying but doing so in a strategic way. Instead of mere willingness, drive involves wanting and pursuing. How we talk about drive in our stories differs from how we talk about hard work in important ways.

When she was in high school in a working-class community just outside Philadelphia, June's desire to "get out" was so evident that it was noted in the school yearbook. Her neighborhood wasn't bad, but it wasn't good either. "There wasn't this vision that there was more," June recalled. The community produced people who could get a job and stay put. But June had "an adventurous spirit." She wanted something else. And this was a big reason why, she says, she was the one from the neighborhood who left to go to college, moved to New York, and started her own business.

I heard tales like this multiple times. Drive was presented as a differentiator between people in otherwise similar situations. Wilson had grown up in the Philadelphia projects and left his peers there behind because, he said, he had a little more drive. Carl, the owner of the contracting company, said his brother made more money than he did because "he has more of a drive."

Unlike hard work, which may or may not actually pay off, drive was almost always brought up to explain success. Drive is understood to be effective. Drive also differs from hard work in that it is sometimes presumed to be innate, whereas hard work is generally framed as a behavior under individual control. Relatedly, hard work is almost always treated as praiseworthy. With drive, the moral dimension sometimes drops out.

"There's lots of things that I could have done that would have made me more successful, I guess, if I'd shown more initiative and energy," explained Rick, a retired military intelligence analyst, about why he didn't go further in his career. He did not regard this as an indictment of his character, however. "I feel satisfied," he said. "I've never been a type-A person. . . . I never felt the need to be first in everything." He believed he had worked hard, but not been very ambitious, and said that was fine.

Gary, the owner of a retail store, loved to sing and belonged to a choir. Music was his passion, he said, but could never have been his career. "I never thought I had the tenacity or drive to make it in the music industry. It's a little bit more cutthroat than what I am," he said. That work required a great deal of self-promotion, and he didn't have it in him. He did not seem to think this was a personal weakness.

Remember that Jesse Jackson was acknowledged to be an ambitious striver whose deservedness was nevertheless doubted by the political press. In Jackson's case, drive was construed as negative. This is because drive is a quality of more ambiguous valence than hard work. A person might be criticized for working hard in pursuit of something bad or wrong, but the problem in that case would be the goal rather than the effort. Drive itself is sometimes presented as bad, and lacking drive is acceptable under some circumstances.

Many observers have noted that drive is frequently regarded in American culture as less desirable in women ("bitchy") and minorities ("uppity") than in white men. I would add that lacking drive is perceived as a character flaw mostly for poor people. People in comfortable circumstances can argue that they have substantial merit without demonstrating drive; for them, hard work is enough. For poor people, lacking drive is itself an indictment.

I don't expect the observation that drive can be framed as good or bad to land as a shock. But I do want to highlight how it demonstrates the complexity of our expectations for ourselves. Effort matters quite a lot in the American understanding of who deserves success. But not all effort is equal. We have varying ideas about where different kinds of effort come from and what they're worth.

"Grit" is similarly nuanced. Angela Duckworth writes that grit "entails working strenuously toward challenges, maintaining effort and interest over years despite failure, adversity, and plateaus in progress."[16] Yvette, a thirty-five-year-old teacher, said that precisely this quality had been crucial in attaining her stable middle-class life. "[I've had] a lot of setbacks. . . . There are some people who aren't able to deal with that, and those setbacks could totally change the trajectory of their lives."

Stan likewise considered himself a "fighter." He had grown up in the projects in North Philadelphia, made it out, became a police officer, and then worked his way up the ranks of Philadelphia-area police departments, he said, in spite of racial discrimination and a general tendency for promotions to be based on affiliation more than ability. He had put up with snubs and disappointments— even once saw an interviewer roll his eyes when he walked into the room. Stan believed he had acquired his fighting spirit, which enabled him to tough all this out, in part because his parents put an emphasis on "coping skills," and in part because he grew up in an environment where fighting was necessary.

Grit is often described as a product of circumstance: people say they acquired toughness from experiences that required toughness of them. But such accounts frequently include an implication that the capacity for grit is *in* you, somewhere, because other people didn't or wouldn't have survived the same trials that forged and/ or demonstrated your backbone. After all, the other people from Stan's neighborhood also grew up in a tough neighborhood.

In this sense, grit occupies a vague sweet spot between innate and acquired the hard way. Exhibiting grit consequently reads as something *you* do, and *you* control, and not because you got lucky in one way or another. It checks a lot of boxes in terms of how Americans think about merit.

And yet when I asked people whether or why they deserved something, the answer was rarely "Yes, because I had grit." Grit was sometimes described as a contributor to success but not generally as a justification for it. Certainly rewards can be earned without grit. Stan, for instance, believed he had earned some of his promotions before he fought for them. His deservedness preceded the application of grit. Grit appears to enhance deservedness but is not automatically associated with it the way hard work is. My best guess is that this is because grit is a response to circumstances outside one's control.

Grit is also a quality that, at least among my interviewees, few people seem to think they lack. Though some interviewees admitted to not working especially hard or having much drive, few said they had insufficient resilience, persistence, or grit. Even among the numerous people I interviewed who were disappointed in their lives and placed the blame at their own feet, no one said, "I'm a quitter." I suspect most people experience their lives as difficult at one point or another and keep going.

Work and effort, then, sit squarely in the center of how we talk about merit, much more so than talent, but they're not straightforward or consistent. Nor is "work" the only thing we have to do to earn a reward in our stories.

Multiple Choice: Decision Making

Someone reading this chapter, somewhere, has already been objecting, saying that *of course* working hard isn't all you have to do to earn a reward. It matters what work you do. Depending on whom you ask, it might not be reasonable to expect a reward for working hard in an MFA program, or at trying to become an NFL player if you are uncoordinated and slow, or at giving predatory loans to poor people. It might not be reasonable to expect a reward if you decline to meet with a potential mentor because you're working hard on an unimportant assignment, or smoke weed the night before a company drug test. The underlying theme in these cases, and the quality we have to think about to understand merit, is decision making.

Consider Erin, a wealthy fifty-something housewife facing the prospect of an empty nest, but without a career to return to. Erin did not feel that she had failed to work hard. In fact, she called herself a "worker bee." Nor did she think she lacked drive. Yet the professional portion of her life was not turning out to her satisfaction, and she had an idea why. "I sort of wish I made different choices," she said. "I really wish I had a career that I could go back to." After college Erin had worked as a broker's assistant, then as an event planner, before dropping out of the workforce to stay home with her children. This meant she had not acquired training or developed an expertise she could now apply. "I'm always talking about going back to work now that the kids are grown," she said. "I'm itching to do something smarter than what I'm doing." Her friends were lawyers, nurses, an occupational therapist. "It's hard to see ahead of you," she said, looking back.

Decisions about what kind of career to pursue, as well as decisions about how to pursue it, surface frequently in our stories as a relevant factor in how much success we enjoy. In my interviews, examples of this ranged from choosing the wrong major in college, to not going to college, to turning down an offer to leave one job for another, to selling the family farm. There were also decisions that occurred outside a person's working life but were nevertheless understood to affect socioeconomic status, like choosing a partner who helped you or held you back, or taking drugs.

But while all of these decisions were understood to be crucial, only some of them were thought of as acts that spoke to a person's merit. Joe, who had worked as a draftsman until the home-building industry collapsed, had clearly made a decision to go into that field, but he didn't feel the choice reflected poorly on him. The industry's fortunes were way beyond his control, and he did not think he could have been expected to foresee them. "I never walked away saying personally I think I could have done anything differently," he told me. "You're just along for the ride."

Joe's explanation helps illustrate how we determine whether to credit or blame someone for a decision or chalk it up to luck. We ask whether the decision maker had decent options, had or should have had access to sufficient information, and applied reasonable values and expectations in making his or her choice. Given the information available to him, Joe felt he had made a reasonable choice about his career path, and thus did not think he deserved the negative consequences that followed. Ronald the handyman, by contrast, regretted not having gone to college but said that because he had been advised to enroll, the decision was his own damn fault.

These judgments are deeply subjective, of course, and so can vary widely, making the question of whether a person is responsible for a given decision another flexible piece of our thinking about merit. I can certainly imagine someone arguing that Ronald shouldn't really fault himself for choosing not to go to college when he was making money working as a contractor and many of his peers were dealing drugs. How many kids would have made that decision under those circumstances? Similarly, I can imagine someone arguing that Joe should have been more attuned to the realities of his own industry. Did he really think there were enough rich people to support all that new construction in the Philadelphia suburbs in 2006? Whether a decision is *on you* is up to you.

In early 2019, shortly after two major digital media companies eliminated over one thousand journalists' jobs, reporters who took to social media to commiserate or advertise their newly available services were inundated with messages offering career advice. "Learn to code," trolls counseled them, repeatedly and in a creative array of meme-y ways. The suggestion, delivered with varying (but usually low) levels of earnestness, aimed to portray pursuing a career in journalism as a *decision* journalists were making despite better available options and with sufficient information, perhaps because their priorities were in the wrong place, or perhaps because they didn't want to put in the work to "learn to code." The fact that few of the "learn to code" posters actually expected journalists to learn to code is beside the point; the phrase worked as a taunt because it was a way of telling the laid-off journalists, "You deserve what you're getting."

Big Spenders and Penny-Pinchers

One particular category of decision making warrants special mention in a discussion of socioeconomic merit: the decision to spend or save. Sara had saved throughout her government career, and the fact that she had done so was an important piece of why she felt she had earned her comfortable retirement. "I don't live above my means," she said when I asked whether she had earned what she had. Frugality was an area in which she felt she had separated herself from some of her peers who were not as financially secure. She told me about friends who lived "lavish lives," and a girlfriend who'd bought, and then lost, a big house. Carl, the contractor, offered a similar explanation. Seated with his wife at his dining room table, he declared, "We never buy anything that we couldn't afford. The only thing we've ever had a mortgage on was when we bought this land for twenty-six thousand dollars." The house in which we sat, he said, "was built piece by piece, two, three years, working on the house. Always cash. Or check, I guess. But you gotta live within your means, and you gotta prepare for the future." Several interviewees who were hard up for money said they didn't deserve any better because they had spent their way into a hole.

Saving up had enabled Carl to build his business, but frugality and profligacy were not typically referenced as practices that helped or hindered people in their professional pursuits. It just explained how much money they had. Harold, who had worked on a county road crew for many years, hadn't made a great deal of money, but he was still proud of what he had done to achieve financial comfort. "It's not so much the money, it's what you do with your money," he said. For much of his adult life he burned coal for heat, until, he said, coal became harder to come by. So he bought a trailer full of logs, split them himself, and heated his home with wood.

For several interviewees who mentioned their spending habits, the rationale was pretty straightforward: you deserve money if you decide to save it and don't if you decide to spend it. I should note, though, that it is very easy to imagine exceptions to this rule. No interviewee described going broke because of a sick child's medical bills, for example, but at least some people would consider destitution undeserved under those circumstances.

One wonders, then, whether Sara's friend with the big house would agree that she had been wasteful to acquire it, or whether someone living in a rental trailer in Carl's community might have some powerful explanation for why she was unable to save the way Carl did. Every few months, it seems, there is a social media scuffle about someone sharing advice on buying a home, paying off student loans, or some other financial matter without appreciating the limitations others face. As I write this, Twitter is buzzing about an article published in *Business Insider* about a thirty-one-year-old who "paid off $220,000 in student loans in 3 years."[17] The thirty-one-year-old took a job at a nonprofit run by her mother and lived in a condo her mother had given her as a gift. Commenters were having a field day mocking the idea that this person's frugality was meritorious. "Pay off your debt with property given to you for free. It's so easy!" wrote one.[18] I'm not suggesting there's no right or wrong in this spat—certainly the critics were correct that there's a financial reality that applies to many people that doesn't apply to this particular thirty-one-year-old. But fights like this keep happening because frugality is accepted as a "good reason" for deservedness without any shared cultural anchor for when it is a reasonable expectation. Then again, the "good reasons" of narrative rationality need not satisfy traditional logical standards. Like other kinds of decisions, whether you deserve the consequences of your spending choices depends on the circumstances—and, crucially, on who is making the call.

Do the Right Thing: Morality

Most of the qualities we consider *deserving* of reward are also presumed to be helpful in *obtaining* reward. Morality is different.

Carl argued that ethical conduct in his professional life had in fact helped him become successful. "As long as you don't cheat 'em, you got 'em," he said, by way of explaining how he built his customer base. More frequently, moral choices and/or ethical behavior such as compassion and honesty are treated as unrelated to success—even unhelpful. Mark, the forty-four-year-old grocery store employee, felt that his efforts to be kind and caring to people around him had backfired, at least in his personal life: "All it has done is open me up to be taken advantage of." Susan felt that her honesty had hindered her in her pursuits.

Whether or not morality helps you succeed, though, people treated it as necessary in order to deserve success. For instance, Daniel, an artist, had fallen into gangbanging in his teens. At sixteen and seventeen, he said, he was illegally selling guns, stealing cars, and getting into big brawls. When I spoke to him, he was nearing forty, had been out of that life for a long time, and felt that he worked hard and contributed to the lives of those around him for relatively little pay. When I asked whether he felt that he was earning more than he got, however, he said no, because he was still balancing his moral ledger. He had worked hard, but he viewed it as "repayment for a lot of years of bad stuff, a lot of years of destruction," he said. "I owe a lot, spiritually and figuratively."

Multiple other interviewees cited a moral component to their calculations of what they deserved. "A lot of people are taught to prosper," Sara said, "but how did you get your money?" In her thirty years of government work, including some spent working with delinquent youth, she felt that she had contributed to the greater good. This supported her sense that she had earned her comfortable retirement. A twenty-seven-year-old drug dealer told me that she had helped people through what she called her "trade," bringing them relief, and considered this a contribution deserving of reward. James, a fireman, said that although he had worked hard and done a good job, he probably didn't deserve his good life because he had driven drunk too many times. Pam tried to pay back her privileges by helping her massage clients at an affordable price.

Moral behavior, both in the workplace and out of it, is viewed generally as a quality under individual control (with the exception of one interviewee who described it as innate, saying that if you watch little kids play, "by eight years old you can tell everybody . . . whether or not your child is gonna be in jail"). Consequently, acting immorally, by cheating, cutting corners, or treating people poorly, could reduce your deservedness, and acting morally could enhance it, especially if your work could be framed as a social contribution. But it's important to note that "I never cheated" or even "I was scrupulous and ethical" tend not to be cited as a *primary* explanation for why someone deserves success the way hard work often is. I came to think of morality as a prerequisite for merit, a bar someone had to clear to become deserving.

How one clears that bar is one of the questions we fight about most in debates over meritocracy. Does paying employees the minimum wage disqualify a CEO from deserving generous compensation? If you work in marketing for a pharmaceutical company with questionable ethical practices, do you deserve your paycheck? Do college professors deserve a middle-class living if their schools' graduates are mired in debt with poor job prospects? These judgments, like so many others we've seen, are at the discretion of the individual storyteller.

The Meaning of Merit

To recap: The talents you are born with are out of your control, and we'd like to think they really matter only if you work hard. Working hard is under your control, but it may not always pay off, plus the ambition that fuels certain kinds of hard work might *not* be under your control, and hard work isn't always admirable, depending on what decisions you make. Decision making is sometimes under your control, depending on the circumstances of a decision, but certain crucial decisions such as how to use your money are deeply disputed cultural territory. Morality is important, but not sufficient to deserve reward, and no one agrees what it is. And that, my friends, is the American definition of merit.

Individual interviewees were not always this confused or contradictory about what qualities deserve reward. What I'm highlighting here is the fact that the generally agreed-upon terms of what it takes to earn something in American culture are not very well developed or agreed upon. I would argue that the main principles that hold most interviewees' personal philosophies together are these: We exercise individual agency by making *choices*. Then we pay for the things we deserve with *time* and *struggle*.

Remember Kia, who suspected that if her brother had been raised the way she was, his life would have been different? He wouldn't have been as lazy, and he would have encountered different opportunities. I said this sounded like he was dealt a bad hand. She disagreed.

"I don't know if that was a bad hand, though," she said. "You were given things in life. You had a choice to make. . . . He can't blame my parents forever. At what point do a person take ownership of their actions?"

"I think it's really confusing," I pushed, annoyingly. "Because we want to say a person should take ownership, but then we also say who he is was created by [his parents], right?"

"In part," she said.

"What's the other part?" I asked.

"When do he step up to do what he's supposed to?" she replied.

I actually wanted *Kia's* answer to this question. So I turned the question around and asked when she stepped up. "You're talking about him failing to ever make the right choice," I said. "When did you start making the right choice?"

She thought for a moment.

"We had like a laundry room," she said. "And everybody put their clothes in there. I was separating and washing clothes at eleven and twelve years old. Everyone's clothes. The only thing my mother didn't have me doing was cooking, because she didn't want me to touch her stove. I had to clean her bathroom, clean the whole kitchen after everybody eat. She didn't play, you had to sweep *and* do the stove. Oh my god. I used to—he didn't have to do *anything!* So I mean . . . even in middle school, I played sports, I had straight As. I was always into school. I didn't need no one to say, 'You have to get this.' I was gonna earn it, because that's what I wanted."

I took from this that Kia and her brother were just different, and maybe it didn't matter why. There was a sense in these conversations that at a certain point, you have to put aside existential questions. One of the confusing aspects of the American notion of merit is that both nature and nurture can reasonably be construed as luck. You have control over neither your genes nor your formative experiences. If merit is "the result of the exercise of some quality of ours, and possession of that quality is not caused by factors beyond our control," writes Robert Simon,[19] where exactly are meritorious attributes supposed to come from?

Our answer, ultimately, is "Who cares?"

This is not to say we never excuse mistakes, obviously, just that we don't articulate a coherent philosophy about when it is appropriate to do so. We take stock of advantages and disadvantages, decide whether they were reasonable, and after that, we look at people's *choices*, as Kia says—and here I mean something broader than discrete decisions like what field to enter or whom to marry. I mean also gradual, ongoing choices like the choice to work hard or the choice to behave ethically or the choice to want something more. These choices are what we hold ourselves accountable for "at some point."

The reason talent doesn't deserve reward is that it doesn't involve individual choice. It's just there, until we choose to develop or apply it. The reason we don't worry about whether grit, drive, or even a predisposition toward hard work might be innate is that they appear to involve choice in any case.

The choices that most *deserve reward* are ones that involve the expenditure of time or the absorption of unpleasantness. Hard work involves choosing to spend your time and comfort (not just work but "hard" work). Drive involves making these choices in a more targeted way, and sometimes involves the risk of further potential sacrifice. Grit involves making the choices over and over, spending more time, enduring more struggle. Frugality means forfeiting enjoyment. We pay for deservedness with our most fundamental resources: our time and our comfort. If our behavior while we spend these resources is morally acceptable, we have merit. If our behavior is morally admirable, all the better.

"I Don't Believe in Suffering Just So You Can Succeed"

Now think of all the aspects of individual merit that are open for interpretation: Whether a star is innately talented or worked to develop her talent. Whether a corporate lawyer or a furniture mover works hard. Whether a graduate student should have known not to get that degree. Whether the millennial should forgo the avocado toast. Whether it's immoral to sell drugs. Even whether you are responsible for the traits instilled in you by your parents.

This flexible definition of merit, I suspect, explains and/or causes a great many of the debates in American culture about people getting more or less than they deserve. With such murky standards for how a person earns reward, it's no surprise that we would reach different conclusions about who deserves what and evaluate people unfairly—whether going easier on favored groups (white kids who make mistakes deserve a second shot, etc.), going easier on ourselves, or going harder on ourselves in some cases. Part of what I'm going to argue at the end of this book is that a flexible construction of merit is inevitable, and so instead of defining it better, we should prioritize it less.

The other thing that jumped out at me about the way my interviewees talked about merit in their lives is that it was so different from how we tend to define merit in institutions, in theory, and even in certain aspects of culture. Our version of merit is not actually consistent with meritocracy.

In a meritocracy, it's okay for someone to coast on talent. Let's say Doug was just ridiculously smart, everything came easily to him, and he was able to get his PhD and run a real estate business at the same time without breaking a sweat. In a meritocracy, if he's the best man for the job, he still gets the reward—regardless of whether someone else put in more time or struggled more. Why does talent not count as merit but nevertheless deserves reward in a theoretical meritocracy? I think it's because we conceive of a meritocratic system as a practical proposition and the notion of individual merit as more of an existential one. We know that we can't eliminate the influence of talent practically, but we can dismiss it in contemplating what we deserve.

Along somewhat similar lines, the ambivalence we demonstrate about drive and ambition at the individual level doesn't register nearly as much at the institutional or theoretical level. In an individual, wanting something for oneself very badly and pursuing it doggedly may be perceived as a sign of a character flaw, a trait to be regarded with suspicion under some circumstances. In many meritocratic contexts, it seems to help. It's why the boss wants to hire the go-getter. It's why the person who aggressively takes credit for the group project gets the promotion.

In certain cultural contexts as well, Americans seem to favor a version of merit that is more friendly to ambition and talent than my interviewees were when speaking about themselves. Ambition is celebrated as an unambiguous virtue everywhere from *Shark Tank* to graduation speeches. Our treatment of talent is even more confusing. Schools and companies talk about identifying and cultivating talent; we praise people for being gifted, talented, brilliant, etc.; Donald Trump, among others, insults people by saying they have "no talent"; we enable and permit talented people to get away with various atrocious behaviors so that we may go on enjoying and/or benefiting from the fruits of their talents.

We say we admire hard work and that talent is a secondary consideration, but we certainly don't consistently treat talent as unrelated to success and undeserving of it. We marry hard work. But we love talent.

Josh, a twenty-five-year-old, had dropped out of community college because he was "lazy," he said. After that he worked a string of dead-end jobs in which he said he applied very little effort and in one case just stopped showing up. He thought his bosses had been fair to him for the most part. But Josh didn't feel bad about any of this. "I don't believe in suffering just so you can succeed," he said. He expected his talent, of which he had a fairly high estimate, to carry him through life.

It struck me as very rare for someone to just *say* something like this. We probably all know people who behave this way. But I think few people realize this is their philosophy, and fewer still admit it. It's not a conventional way to represent oneself as having or understanding merit.

Still, I didn't much doubt that Josh was likely to be proven right. By the time he spoke to me, a friend had gotten him into a training program for computer programming, he found that the work came easily to him, and he had gotten a job. He was charismatic, and said his employers liked him. They wouldn't mind that he cut corners if he did the job well enough.

From a narrative perspective, then, Josh was an exception. But in practice I suspect he's closer to the rule.

4

Merit without the -ocracy

Toward the end of each interview, I asked people two related questions. I said that America is built in part on the idea that people here end up about where they deserve to be in their working lives, according to their efforts and abilities. Then I asked people: Have you experienced your life that way? Have you gotten to about where you deserve to be?

Next, I asked the same question but about society instead of about the interviewee. Do you think *other people* for the most part end up about where they deserve in America? How well do you think our country is delivering on its promise?

When I asked Doug the Rich Guy these questions, he said he had ended up in a "pretty accurate" socioeconomic position, given his performance, but that he knows in society at large many opportunities go to people who don't deserve them. He even said he understood the fancy suburb he lived in to be basically about class reproduction. Eric the computer programmer also said he personally had been rewarded fairly in an unfair society. So did Nick the corporate lawyer, Sara the retiree, Jon the "future mayor," Gary the retail store manager, and Deb the former attorney. As I mentioned earlier, Carl the contractor emphasized hard work and personal responsibility throughout his description of his own achievements—"Endeavor to improve myself is what I did"; "My whole life, all I needed was a job. Never on unemployment"; "You gotta paddle your own canoe. Whatever it takes"—and then surprised me by turning around and answering my question about society by saying, "There's not a whole lot of opportunity for a lot of people. . . . There needs to be a job."

These were all people who felt relatively successful. But several interviewees who felt *un*successful also said they had gotten what they deserved—had earned their failures—though they thought most unsuccessful people did not. Susan the office manager believed she had no one to blame but herself for her disappointments, but said that in general, luck was a decisive factor in people's lives. Ronald the handyman said that society was clearly unfair to black males, but that he, a black male, had gotten a fair shake and screwed up.

Then there were people who said that society is basically fair, but they personally got lucky or unlucky. James the fireman was one of these. "Ninety percent of people land up where they [should be]," but in his case, he said, "I've been lucky." For example, some years earlier he had purchased a property that had since appreciated in value considerably, a development for which he took little credit. "I definitely wasn't a strategist and I couldn't even spell it," he told me. He would be able to retire and live on savings and Social Security, and because of that, he said, "I feel like I'm ahead of where I think I should be."

In some senses, sixty people is a lot of people to interview. But for a yes-or-no question about public opinion like "Do Americans think they live in a meritocracy?" an unscientific sample of this size is not enough to draw confident conclusions. What I want to explore in this chapter is not the vote count on these questions (for the record, many more interviewees said they got what they deserved than not, and most said Americans don't live in a meritocracy), but rather the logic that seemed to guide interviewees' responses. One of the key patterns was how *independent* the evaluation of an individual could be from the evaluation of society at large. What you said about whether you personally deserved what you had didn't depend much on whether you believed you lived in a meritocracy.

Social scientists have found that the way a person thinks about others and the way she thinks about herself need not line up.[1] For one thing, people have a lot more information about our own lives than we do about everyone else's, and so our explanations of each are likely to differ. For another, as James Kluegel and Eliot Smith say, people do not necessarily feel a need to achieve "cognitive consistency" in our beliefs, and one of the areas in which we appear to forgo consistency is in our thinking about the relationship between the "dominant ideology" of individualism, which says that we mostly end up where we should, and the challenging theme of "social liberalism," which says that no, right now we don't.[2] Rather than choose one perspective or the other, we "layer" them, applying elements of each situationally.

Still, the precise thinking at work here is curious. Meritocracy isn't a zero-sum game. Economies can grow, and socioeconomic rewards are too subjective for one person's gain always to be another's loss. (Prestige in particular is not a finite resource. You receiving more has little bearing on my prospects.) But theoretical meritocracy is a system—a *competitive* system—with interdependent parts, and what happens to some of those parts has implications for the others. If some people are excluded from certain opportunities, it makes life easier for potential competitors. And yet we say that what I earn has not much to do with you.

A couple of years ago I was speaking about this project with a tenured professor (in other words, someone with an enviable job), who said something to the effect of "I think I've earned my position. I just want more people to have the opportunity to do the same." I find this impulse admirable. But it should be said that if more people had a robust opportunity to earn, say, a position as a tenured professor, it might become harder to become a tenured professor, and this particular tenured professor might not make the cut. This doesn't mean she doesn't actually deserve her job. It means that deserving her job, by her standard, does not require a meritocratic process. We often release ourselves from the requirements of meritocracy when thinking about our own lives.

We accomplish this in large part through precisely the kinds of stories and explanations we've been examining. In chapter 1, we saw that American stories don't take meritocracy for granted but rather ask in individual cases whether a person, even an extremely successful person, ended up where he or she deserves to be. In chapter 2, we saw how people attempt to account for and explain the role of external circumstances in their lives in order to evaluate their individual contributions. In chapter 3, we considered which individual contributions are deemed worthy of reward.

Faced with the questions of whether we ultimately earned what we have and/or deserve to be where we are, we put these pieces together. This process allows us to nod toward meritocracy without bowing to it. And the standard we usually use to make our determinations of individual deservedness, I would argue—the "good reasons" in our narratives for saying we deserve something—have more to do with *merit* than *meritocracy*.

We require ourselves to display positive individual qualities, and explain away the system in which they are displayed.

Enough Is Enough

Erica changed her mind in the middle of telling me whether she earned it. A twenty-four-year-old black woman studying to be an EMT, she had made clear throughout our conversation that she was not impressed with herself. Erica came from a middle-class family, and had attended a high school that required her to pass a test to gain admission. "I think I just had a good day, honestly," she said. "I just kinda got lucky." Then she went to an elite college (graduating, she said, was "not really an accomplishment") and got a job doing clerical work. Her EMT training was part of her effort to figure out if she wanted to go to medical or nursing school. In this respect, she said, she felt behind her friends, many of whom were enrolling in PhD or master's programs, though she seemed secure in the expectation that she would prove successful eventually.

Erica regarded herself as very much a product of circumstance. She attributed her situation to her family's support, and upon further prompting to her friends and to the grace of God. She said she couldn't think of any disadvantages she had experienced and didn't seem eager to discuss the subject. (Later she would say that black people and women suffer discrimination in America; she just didn't view that discrimination as an important part of her own experience.) When I asked her if she had earned her position, she initially said, "I can't really say I've earned it. I kind of feel like I haven't done anything to earn it."

A moment later, though, when I brought this up again, she changed her mind.

"Well, I feel bad about [saying] that," she said. "I think I've earned what I have, actually. Erase what I just said."

I asked how she had earned it.

"Just staying focused on getting an education," she replied. "I definitely worked hard." Earlier, she had also said that the part of her life she controlled was "just doing it. Just carrying it out, not giving up on myself. . . . I attribute that to myself I guess."

Erica had initially said that, because circumstances had largely placed her in her situation, her personal contributions were not enough ("I haven't done anything"). Then she decided that, actually, she had tried rather hard, and this was sufficient to say she had earned it.

The process Erica appeared to go through of evaluating the role of circumstances in her life and attempting to evaluate her personal contribution, asking whether it was enough to earn what she had, was something I heard over and over. It is true, as Kluegel and Smith say, that Americans don't view individual and external explanations as alternatives, in the sense that one cancels out the other. Both always exist and usually matter. We use our stories to contextualize the individual within the external, and then make a case for our contribution's sufficiency or inadequacy.

The question is, with so much disagreement about what constitutes an advantage or disadvantage in American life today, and so much muddiness around the matter of what it means to do something on one's own, what if anything can be reliably said about what it means to do "enough" to earn what one has?

That's what I want to wrestle with in this chapter. But first, I want to deal with those friends of Erica's in graduate programs who made her feel behind, because Erica might have reached a different conclusion about what she'd earned if she looked around and decided she was doing very well, or very poorly, rather than just okay. Which is to say, before we examine what people think is "enough" to earn what they have, we have to consider how they take stock of what they have.

S-u-c-c-e-s-s, That's the Way We Spell Success

"I don't have any kids, a lot of people my age have kids, so I'm successful in that respect," said Josh, the twenty-five-year-old college dropout when I asked if he considered himself successful. It won't surprise you to learn that success and failure, like so much else here, are subjective notions. Some other interviewees around Josh's age pointed to the fact that they didn't have kids as a reason they considered themselves *un*successful. I was particularly struck by Leonard, a fifty-two-year-old catering manager from North Philly, who explained that he was successful because he had been to the top of the tallest buildings in the city on catering gigs. "I can't believe they let me up here," he recalls thinking.

Different interviewees' constructions of success included economic comfort (factors like income, savings, home ownership, ability to pay for an education, and more), prestige, gratification, family stability, and carceral status. Interpretations of what represented success in most of these categories varied broadly. For many younger interviewees, my question about success actually became a question about trajectory toward success, and how well positioned they were to achieve desirable things in the future. It is important to note that success was not a yes-or-no proposition; interviewees understood it as a continuum. In explaining that he had done okay but not *that* well, for instance, Josh said that he was pleased not to be living in North Philly, ten minutes away, but that "this is, like, the hood still, it's not like a super-nice neighborhood."

That said, there were two formulations interviewees reached for repeatedly when explaining how successful they felt, and those tell us something about American ideas of success.

The Starting Line and Keeping Up with the Joneses

Kia: Have I beat some of the odds? Yes. I came from North Philly, where it was guns, drugs around me every day. I'm no longer in that environment.

James: Coming from pretty minuscule upbringing and surroundings—my mom really struggled raising five kids and didn't get any support from my biological father—I just feel like I have more than most people that I grew up with. I did a little better than most people I grew up with.

Rebecca: I was born into a situation where I had a lot of benefits that a lot of people don't have, and if I hadn't had those, statistically speaking, I wouldn't be where I am. I have no way of knowing exactly what my life would be like, but one of my best friends . . . she is at least professionally, in many ways at the same level or even beyond me, but she was a refugee. So the delta for her is much greater. So I don't think there's a black-and-white answer to that, because I can see where she had to start, and where she is, and where I had to start, and where I am, and we're basically at the same point.

The socioeconomic trajectory most commonly associated with meritocratic stories is, of course, rags to riches. But when people talk about their own lives, they also tell rags-to-not-rags stories, riches-to-more-riches stories, and even riches-to-not-riches stories. In short, many of us calibrate success in relation to starting point, asking whether we've made appropriate progress given where we began.

The most common starting point my interviewees referenced when explaining their success was socioeconomic status, as we see in all three examples just quoted, and others throughout this book: people evaluate success in the context of their parents' jobs and finances, the neighborhoods where they grew up, and the educational opportunities afforded them.

But there are other kinds of "starting point" too, some having little to do with socioeconomic status. In her book *New Jersey Dreaming*, Sherry Ortner goes back and interviews people from her high school class. She talks to one woman who had been an excellent student, and "by most accounts would be seen as quite successful," but "felt embarrassed to see people from high school, because 'she didn't live up to her potential.'"[3]

Among my interviewees, Samantha, a twenty-seven-year-old drug dealer, described her mental health as a kind of "starting point" against which she gauged success. A lot of people in her situation, she said, don't make it as far as she did. Another interviewee implied that her success needed to be measured in relation to her ADD, although Mark, who worked at a grocery store, said he had ADD but didn't want to treat the condition as an "excuse." We saw in profiles of athletes that natural talent can be used as a sort of starting point against which success can be measured (Larry Bird was successful considering that he couldn't jump, etc.), but no interviewees said anything to the effect of "I should have done better considering how smart I am."

Whatever the starting point, though, the basic logic was that where you "start" serves as an anchor for expectations about how far you should go. For some of the folks who focused on socioeconomic status, this just meant that "success" was represented by upward mobility across generations. Several interviewees said they had been successful because they had done better than their parents, and a couple of people who felt unsuccessful pointed to the fact that they had done worse. The basic expectation of class advancement (or at least maintenance) appeared to hold even among people under forty who should not, statistically speaking, expect such generational progress.

In other cases, expectations were measured not against a general sense of class status but against specific individuals: kids from the neighborhood, like the ones James the fireman talked about, or siblings. Comparing oneself to childhood peers, I suspect, is effectively an effort to narratively "control" for socioeconomic factors like class, geography, and race (because of the segregation of many American neighborhoods and schools) in evaluating an individual's success. Comparing oneself to siblings isolates individual contribution even more by controlling for family too. A thirty-seven-year-old woman who believed she had gone further professionally than her siblings said she had done so because she had more grit.

Measurements of success are not always anchored to the past. Some interviewees compared themselves to contemporary friends and colleagues, gauging their achievements against a sense they derived from peer groups about what is possible. Recall Susan saying that "lots of people do that, raise a kid and have a job and do it all," when I asked why she blamed herself for failing to build a satisfying career when she had been busy as a single parent. Social media in general and Facebook in particular came up in several interviews as a tool for making these comparisons. (Or thrusting them in our faces: there is a well-documented "compare and despair" phenomenon that Facebook is understood to exacerbate.) Chris Hayes writes in *Twilight of the Elites* about what he calls "fractal inequality,"[4] wherein wealthy people regard themselves as middle class because they compare themselves only to wealthier people, and wealthier people compare themselves only to wealthier people still, and so on until we reach Jeff Bezos, who perhaps might admit that he's rich.

Again, because success is such a subjective notion, these comparisons can have unpredictable results. Deb, the former lawyer who had taken up a different line of work, knew attorneys who made twenty to thirty times as much as she did. But, she said, "when I talk to other attorneys I'm like, wow, I'm really lucky to not be you. You're miserable and boring." She thought many of the attorneys envied her.

The temptation to evaluate success by comparing oneself to others can be very strong. Consider, for example, Daniel the artist, who told me he thought that outcomes in life are "mostly random," and that because of this, he was trying to stop comparing himself to other artists, a practice he described as basically an epidemic in his community. "Artists . . . go to other artists' websites—people that they admire, are their heroes, or they admire something about them, but probably in a similar age range, but have more success. And they go on their website and they watch their videos and they read the reviews and they go, 'Oh, I wish I had that too.' For hours." This habit, he said, just made people feel bad. Daniel had decided to "stop looking at other people's markers of success." Then he explained why: "Their starting points were different. All of our starting points were different."

Daniel wanted to quit comparing. But to justify this decision, he appeals to the logic of comparison. He can't compare where he is in a race because the starting points were unfair—not because there isn't a race in the first place.

I don't mean to suggest that success is *always* conceived either as progress over time, comparison to a peer group, or some combination of the two. Some interviewees defined success simply as a situation they would find satisfactory. Vicki, a thirty-one-year-old woman who had worked as a vet tech but was unemployed when we spoke, said success for her would mean having her own house, a job, and providing for her kids without problems or assistance. It didn't matter in her description what anyone else achieved or acquired. But the fact that these two formulations surfaced repeatedly is noteworthy, because both draw on meritocratic premises: thinking of success in terms of progress over time draws on the premise of social mobility, and measuring success through comparison draws on the premise of competition. For many of us, then, whether we say we live in a meritocracy or not, the ways we talk about success conjure the ideal of meritocracy. But real life is not ideal, and we know it.

Flexing

Paul, who got a job working for his father's company despite being initially unqualified, says that he has done enough at this point to justify his position. Thomas, who came up "rugged" and says he was mistreated by a racist system, concludes that in the end his mistakes are his, and perhaps enough for him to deserve spending his life in and out of jail. Pam, meanwhile, got her own business off the ground while providing her service at an affordable price. She characterized her role in this achievement this way: "I was a part of it, I was trying really hard," she said. "I wasn't a fuckup." But her success was "all about basically money"—meaning the family money that enabled her climb. She probably didn't do enough to deserve to be where she is, she concluded. Jeff had grown up in a prominent family, and his name and connections had helped him become a successful businessman. He felt that he had done *more* than enough to justify his position but was disadvantaged "because of government intervention." As he explained, "The more money that I make, the more goes to the government."

All of these people, I would argue, make arguments about their deservedness that are *coherent* by American standards. In other words, you might say that one or another of them is wrong, but you wouldn't say any of them is completely out of touch with contemporary American culture. The meaning of "enough" is sufficiently flexible to accommodate each of their conclusions.

Our ideas about what it means to earn or deserve something are so flexible, I think, for two main reasons. The first is simply the bigness of life and the subjectivity of experience. We all anchor our worldview to what we hear, see, and know. We've seen this numerous times already. What seems like an advantage to me might not to you, what feels like hard work to you might not to me, etc. We have different ideas about what it means to do *enough* to deserve reward because we have vastly different understandings of what we've actually done in our lives.

The second reason for our flexibility is that in turning our lives into stories and asking whether we've done enough, we find ways to avoid using the standard of societal meritocracy to evaluate ourselves. Remember that a meritocracy is "a social system as a whole in which individuals get ahead and earn rewards in direct proportion to their individual efforts and abilities."[5] Consider:

- Fortunate interviewees described earning advantages retroactively. After all, being born with an advantage wasn't under their control; all they could control was what they did with those advantages. But in a meritocratic system, it doesn't make sense to earn advantages retroactively, because large advantages make a process unmeritocratic regardless of subsequent admirable behavior.

- Several interviewees said that they didn't deserve something if they got it because of sheer talent, because talent wasn't under their control. But in a meritocratic system, if you were talented enough to outperform other people without trying as hard, you would still merit the reward.
- Several interviewees evaluated success in relation to starting point, saying they had done well considering where they started. But in a meritocratic system, all levels of achievement should be roughly equally available to people from all backgrounds.

This is not to say that people don't take meritocratic standards into consideration when thinking about what we've earned as individuals. The fact that we feel the need to grapple with advantages, disadvantages, and starting points shows we are profoundly influenced by the meritocratic premise of equal opportunity. We also ask whether processes were meritocratic in individual instances, and our answers can influence our opinion of whether we earned a specific job, an award, an admissions spot, etc.

But ultimately, we don't hold ourselves to a standard of societal meritocracy in evaluating our lives—and not because we lie to ourselves and say we live in a meritocracy. An individual earning what he has in a functioning meritocracy might be our ideal, but meritocracy isn't under individual control, and so we explain away deviations from that ideal and hold ourselves to more individual standards.

Those individual standards vary widely, but if one were to characterize them, they would be better understood as "merit" than as "meritocracy." We want to know whether we've displayed sufficient positive qualities deserving of reward—such as hard work, determination, good decision making, drive, and morality—in order to determine whether we are deserving of our outcomes, and the system in which those qualities are expressed is a secondary concern.

Through this lens, the "good reasons" we see popping up in our stories begin to seem more coherent:

- If your standard is merit rather than meritocracy, it can make sense to earn advantages retroactively, because you are exhibiting a positive quality.
- If your standard is merit rather than meritocracy, it can make sense to eliminate talent from considerations about deservedness if you think talent is unearned.
- If your standard is merit rather than meritocracy, it can make sense to hold yourself accountable for your mistakes regardless of whether the rich kids from the other side of the tracks made many, many more mistakes than you.
- If your standard is merit rather than meritocracy, it can make sense to evaluate success in the context of starting point if doing so gives you a better sense of what an individual brought to the table.

The assessment of whether you have adequate merit, much more than an assessment of whether we live in a meritocracy, is flexible, and accommodating of many different conclusions, from a guy like Paul whose father "spoiled the shit out of his kids" but who says he earned his job with his dad's company to a guy like Thomas who "came up rugged" but says he should have just paid a racist ticket.

What about people like Pam and Jeff, who concluded that they got more or less than they should have because of societal unfairness? Were they applying a standard of meritocracy in evaluating what they deserved? What about the multiple black interviewees who said, matter-of-factly, that racism had held them back relative to white peers?

Pointing to systemic unfairness as an explanation for your situation is not exactly unheard of in American life. The "We Are the 99 Percent" movement that accompanied Occupy Wall Street included a Tumblr page of first-person narratives amounting to precisely that: people describing meritorious behaviors and decisions such as working long hours and living frugally that didn't lead to just reward because of undeserved misfortune such as health care crises and their associated costs.

People who make these arguments are indeed appealing to meritocratic impulses. But if you look closely at the particulars of their stories, their message tends to be that merit has not been met by a reasonable, adequate reward, *not* that a fair (or fair-ish) system is required for them to get what they deserve. When someone says that she works two jobs and can't afford her medical bills, she is citing a lack of decency, not a lack of meritocracy. Similarly, when Philip Mitchell says he thinks things are going to work out in a system that doesn't work, he is not resting his hopes for earned success on the promise of a meritocratic system. The absence of meritocracy does not preclude the possibility of individual deservedness being realized.

"Yes, yes," said Diana, a twenty-six-year-old who worked at an afterschool program, when I asked whether she had earned her success. "This is a hard question because I know that people . . . they can be successful and not have earned it, and people can not be successful and it has nothing to do with whether they've earned it or didn't. All I can say is that I've worked really hard." Diana believes she has enough merit regardless of the state of American meritocracy.

Now, on the one hand, this capacity of ours to believe in meritocracy without *really believing* in meritocracy can be understood as a problem—and it is, in several ways. On the other hand, it introduces an intriguing possibility: if we don't really believe in meritocracy, maybe we don't have to behave like we believe in meritocracy.

5

What's Deserve Got to Do with It?

L et's talk again about Ivanka Trump, because after all, she may be president before all is said and done. In early 2019 she made the following observation about what most Americans want: "I don't think most Americans, in their heart, want to be given something. . . . People want to work for what they get."[1]

The comment was received poorly in certain quarters. "SELF AWARENESS ALERT," tweeted Kenneth Vogel of the *New York Times*.[2] "Has Ivanka Trump ever had a job that her father did not give her?" asked the *Washington Post*'s Eugene Scott.[3] "Ivanka Trump, Famous Nepotism Hire, Says People Want to Work for What They Get," read a *New York Magazine* headline.[4] *The Daily Show* highlighted an episode from one of Trump's books wherein she and her brothers couldn't attract any customers to their lemonade stand and so sold their goods to the family's staff instead. "When life gives you lemonade, sell it to the staff" was the punch line.[5] Trump was well and truly dragged.

But here's the thing: she knows. In *The Trump Card,* in the midst of all her claims and disclaimers about her good fortune and what she had earned, Trump offers this Grand Unifying Theory of Ivanka Trump: "My parents set the bar high for me and my brothers. They gave us a lot, it's true, but they expected a lot in return.

And you can be sure we didn't rise to our positions in the company by any kind of birthright or foregone conclusion."[6]

One consequence of Americans' flexible, individualized, and narrativized idea of deservedness is that basically anyone can conclude whatever they want about what they deserve. We may be more or less able to persuade others of our conclusion, and Trump is an extreme enough case that she struggles in this regard. But whether by allowing her to persuade herself, allowing her to persuade enough of the people around her, or simply providing a permission structure for bullshit, flexible merit is enabling for people like Ivanka Trump. It allows them to claim deservedness without requiring them to compete fairly.

Having said that, I'm not sure how much it matters that Ivanka Trump claims to have earned her success. It's laughable and obnoxious, but I suspect most people can see through it, and anyway, what would change if Trump suddenly admitted what her life has really been like? Would she support living wage legislation? If she did, would anyone care?

There's another dynamic at play here, though, not in Trump's conclusion but in the implicit advancement of certain key premises by both Trump and her critics: that earning reward through merit is *plausible* and *good*, and that whether someone has done that is *knowable*. Trump tries to win admiration by claiming that she is close enough to the meritocratic ideal of a person who earned success. Her critics attempt to deny her this admiration by showing just how much she deviates from that ideal. In both cases, the ideal itself goes unchallenged. No one questions whether someone really can earn a socioeconomic reward, or whether we have any idea who has. Criticism of Trump might even be understood as a celebration of meritocracy, seeing as how it positions the ideal as a preferable contrast to the fraudulent heiress. By implication, inequality remains justifiable *if it's done right*. This is a crucial consequence of our fluid, flexible idea of deservedness.

In her book *Against Meritocracy*, which deserves credit (ahem) for reinstating some of the original skeptical flavor to analysis of the meritocratic ideal, the sociologist Jo Littler writes that meritocracy needs to be understood as an ideology, and that ideologies always involve "instabilities" and "struggles over meaning."[7] What we see when we look at how merit is understood to work in the lives of individuals is that the instability is key to selling the idea. Meritocratic ideology wins Americans over because many of us perceive meritocracy to be efficient, fair, and sensible, but also because it deals so adeptly with challenging evidence and varying interpretations. If the existence of someone like Ivanka Trump caused us to doubt whether meritocracy is possible or desirable, if every person who succeeded with an advantage had to forfeit the dignity of "earning" success, if everyone who *didn't* succeed had to concede that their failure was their own damn fault, meritocracy would be a much less popular proposition. Instead, our narrative approach focuses energy on divining which advantages and disadvantages matter and determining who actually accomplished something on their own. The journey is the destination, as it were.

So perhaps we are living through a period of backlash against American meritocracy. When in September 2017 then–Speaker of the House Paul Ryan tweeted, "In our country, the condition of your birth does not determine the outcome of your life. This is what makes America so great,"[8] the statement, which years ago might have passed as a platitude, was widely derided. "False," read one reply. "In America, the zip code of a person's birth can predict educational attainment and life expectancy with a high degree of accuracy."[9] This species of rejoinder comes from the left, but the contemporary American right, and Trumpism in particular, shot through as it is with disdain for elites and experts, also displays a healthy contempt for the pretense that we live in a meritocracy. Fallout from the COVID-19 pandemic appears likely to strengthen the sense that economic success lies outside of individual control, at least initially.

But backlash against the idea that we live in a meritocracy only rarely causes us to oppose or even question meritocracy itself. At the societal level, as Daniel Markovits observes, complaints about consequences of America's "meritocratic" system, such as inequality, tend to be followed by calls for a better-executed meritocracy, featuring the elimination of obviously unmeritocratic practices such as nepotism, discrimination, and unequal opportunity. Under meritocracy's spell, "hypercompetitive admissions tournaments or Stakhanovite work hours become really wrong only when they discriminate against minorities or working mothers, or mask the operation of insider networks and cultural capital, rather than because they are simply, directly, or generally inhumane."[10]

At the individual level, I suspect, the backlash has mostly resulted in those people most keenly attuned to the unmeritocratic nature of society weighing external factors more heavily in their explanations of individual success or failure. Some of my interviewees, for example, prominently cited privilege, help, or luck in describing how they got to where they are. Recall Laura, the twenty-seven-year-old with a wealthy father, saying of herself, "Money outweighs and trumps so much else." A twenty-six-year-old medical student from an upper-class suburb similarly said she viewed her professional achievements and those of her peers as almost entirely a function of socioeconomic status; she also suspected that being black had helped her in undergraduate and graduate admissions. A version of this perspective is evident outside the world of privilege-checking educated liberals as well. Recall Joe, who had concluded after his industry collapsed that he was "just along for the ride." He was a Trump supporter.

I can't say with authority that there are more people who think this way now than there used to be, but my impression is that this sort of outlook is in part a component of the current cultural environment—the skepticism toward the system, the contempt toward elites. I do feel confident saying that among my interviewees, this view was more common with younger adults than older ones. This could be because people become more comfortable saying they've caused their own outcomes as they get older and just *do more stuff* to influence their own lives. I also think it's likely that the view reflects millennial culture and the socioeconomic realities that helped form it. And as I noted in chapter 2, I think more people will consider their working lives getting upended by a pandemic as sufficiently outside their control to conclude that they're just along for the ride.

Even among people who seemed to have internalized a backlash against meritocracy and worked it into their narratives, though, there was generally little pushback against the idea that earning one's achievements was possible and desirable, and that some people can and do. There was little pushback against the meritocratic *ideal*. Now, I should offer a disclaimer here. I was the one, in many cases, who introduced the premise that someone could earn an outcome: I asked interviewees whether they felt they had earned their station. Interviewees might simply have been following my lead. But most seemed to have considered the question of earned and deserved success before and wished to be able to claim it.

Our vague, flexible notion of merit enables and encourages this commitment to the ideal, even in the face of cultural backlash, by dangling before all of us the *possibility* of meritorious achievement. If it's possible for someone to earn success or failure under the right circumstances, then we can continue to focus on providing the right circumstances, or on evaluating whether and to what extent someone's circumstances and contributions add up to a deserved outcome. This is also why there's no reason to think that Americans would sour on the *ideal* of meritocracy just because a pandemic produces an even more obviously unjust world. We can still tell stories that explain away the effects of COVID-19 in individual cases and pursue "meritocratic" processes in its aftermath.

Only recently in political discourse have calls begun to emerge to see meritocracy itself as a problem. "The afflictions that dominate American life arise not because meritocracy is imperfectly realized, but rather on account of meritocracy itself," Markovits writes. Meritocratic thinking has served to "redeem the very idea of hierarchy," problematically so, because "merit itself is not a genuine excellence but rather—like the false virtues that aristocrats trumpeted in the ancien régime—a pretense, constructed to rationalize an unjust distribution of advantage."[11] Markovits contends that meritocracy does not serve anyone well. To the middle class it denies "dignity and prosperity"; elites it subjects to "self-exploitation" in the form of long work hours and endless anxiety. He suggests "emancipation" from meritocracy. Littler argues that allegedly meritocratic systems inevitably become tautological because of the advantages passed along by winners to their children. Chris Hayes called this the "Iron Law of Meritocracy": "Those who are able to climb up the ladder will find ways to pull it up after them, or to selectively lower it down to their friends, allies, and kin to scramble up."[12] Littler suggests a politics that focuses on equality of outcome rather than opportunity but preserves a belief in human potential.

I want to propose reframing this a bit. My contention is that there is too much that is culturally rooted and, frankly, intuitively appealing about the meritocratic ideal to make disposing of it feasible or desirable.[13] The idea that societies and institutions should aspire to put the right people in the right positions—that someone mechanically inclined should be your electrician, that someone with a strong arm should play quarterback, that someone calm under duress should be your pilot—is sensible on its face. The idea that rewards should be tied to contributions has evolutionary roots (monkeys get angry when they get "unequal pay" for a task),[14] and I don't imagine us being emancipated from this notion anytime soon. Meanwhile, people aren't going to stop putting their own kids first. I don't mean to suggest that Littler or Markovits would disagree with any of these broad points. I'm just outlining why I think we need to work with some version of meritocracy.

But when we look closely at the way people understand our own lives in practice, we see a different opportunity—not to emancipate from meritocracy, or even to execute it more accurately, but to acknowledge its inevitable shortcomings and soften its implications.

"Of the World"

Here are some things that in over sixty hours of conversations about who earned what and why, I never heard anyone say:

> "I deserve better than other people because I'm really talented or lucky, even though I didn't try especially hard."
> "I tried really hard, but I deserved to fail because I never managed to put myself in the right place at the right time."
> "So what if I exploited people? I'm smarter than them. That's why I deserve it."

Certainly Americans regularly behave in ways that suggest we *believe* these things. But I think it matters that we generally don't own them. We say we want reward to be linked to effort and predicated on moral conduct. These are, in my opinion, good things to want: there's a lot to like about the American idea of deservedness. What I meant back in chapter 3 when I said we would do better to "stick with our spouse" when it comes to what we say people deserve is that what we say makes really good sense. The fact that we already say it is an opportunity.

Two more things I never heard anyone say:

> "I achieved success on my own, with no meaningful help or luck."
> "Life in America is completely fair."

When I was working on this book and I would explain it to friends, one talking point I relied on that tended to spark interest was to observe that I didn't think Americans' reputation for thinking we all earn our stations in life was quite right. When you talk to people about this question explicitly, I would say, you find out that most are attuned to the role of things like luck and structure in our lives, and think hard about how to weigh them. One friend responded by saying, "So, they're of the world." This formulation stuck with me, because that's exactly right. People are not dumb; we understand that circumstances matter in life. This is an opportunity too.

The opportunity is to shift political and social focus away from perfecting or replacing meritocracy and instead toward amplifying a reality people already kind of see: meritocracy can be pursued, but even if done relatively well, it doesn't reward the right things— deserve's got nothing to do with it—and moreover, we will never get there. No individual has achieved the meritocratic ideal and none ever will. It's an incoherent vision; life doesn't work that way. Consequently, we should stop acting like life is, can, or will be meritocratic. We should decouple meritocratic achievement from dignity, and instead of fighting for a better chance, fight first for a better life.

We are part of the way there. We already understand reality as a complex interaction between individual and circumstance, and are increasingly observing that circumstance is a very powerful force in this interaction. We already prioritize merit over meritocracy. What we have not done, for the most part, is tell stories that grant individuals dignity in their working lives without trying to figure out how close they come to the meritocratic ideal. But we can do more of that.

Telling New Kinds of Stories

This is the part of the book where I make suggestions. I want to acknowledge before I do that the type of suggestions I'm going to make, about how to tell stories differently in an effort to change American culture, can seem abstract and thus less valuable than, say, a policy agenda. I will mention some policy proposals that might accompany the ideas I'm about to broach, but narrative and myth are the terrain I've been traversing, and so I think this is where I need to plant my flag. I do believe these stories matter. I also want to acknowledge that arguments about how to talk about things, particularly one's own life, are hard to generalize and often presumptuous and condescending. So I want to emphasize that what I'm suggesting here is not that everyone tell every story this way, or that these types of stories are more virtuous than others. What I'm suggesting is that it would be good for Americans to hear these four narrative angles *more*. These are approaches to explaining success, failure, and everything in between that I believe build on Americans' understanding of how life works, but frame the implications differently. If we heard them more often from people explaining their own life trajectories, and from storytellers such as biographers, journalists, etc. discussing the lives of public figures, we could develop a more realistic and healthy relationship to meritocracy.

1. Congratulations to [a group of people].

Jeff is a forty-year-old businessman who was an early supporter of Donald Trump and worked to get him elected, which is to say there are some very important things I didn't admire about Jeff. Frankly he seemed in certain ways like an eighties movie villain: generically good-looking and very comfortable describing the recent firing of an employee. But on the subject of meritocracy he said some things I thought were subversive, in a good way. Jeff came from a prominent family and had used his last name to advance his career. But he neither tried to hide this fact nor downplay it. Instead, when I asked if he was okay with the role his family name had played in his life, he said, "Of course! I think it's fabulous." I asked if it was important to him to have accomplished things on his own. "I don't quite look at it that way," he said. "I look at it as, what are my goals and objectives, and what do I do to get there?"

When I asked him about meritocracy, he replied "I guess I don't think our objective should be to look at it as, should we be a meritocracy? . . . Some things are fair, some things aren't fair. I look at it as, and people say this a lot better than I do, all men are created equal, that's true, but the reality, too, is different people are going to have different circumstances. We can't all be born to billionaires." One of the things he had observed, he told me, is that, with "the people who are really successful, it started probably a couple generations before them. We all want to catch a shooting star these days. And even in my case, I've been the beneficiary of that."

In this regard, Jeff the Trump supporter has found common ground with the cutting edge of left-wing rising stars in Congress, several of whom have made a point of describing their rise to power not as an individual accomplishment but as a collective one. Ilhan Omar honored suffragists on the day of her swearing in. Alexandria Ocasio-Cortez posted on Instagram: "Darkness taught me transformation cannot solely be an individual pursuit, but also a community trust," she wrote. "We must lean on others to strive on our own."

The writer Jill Filipovic published a column arguing that "this refusal to take full individual credit for professional success" is "a very female thing."[15] I think it's true that women are more likely to acknowledge help than men (they did so in my interviews), and there is a debate among researchers about whether more women than men suffer from an "imposter syndrome" wherein they discount their individual roles in their success.[16] But the idea of actually *evaluating* success collectively runs counter to individualistic American assumptions shared by most. People might acknowledge their forebears and thank parents and mentors, but usually to express gratitude for putting them in a position to succeed on their own. We typically try to narrow our explanations of achievement down to the individual.

If we take a cue from Jeff and Ocasio-Cortez, however, we can build on our understanding that success is a group effort by more actively celebrating it as such. Help is good, and should be pursued and enjoyed; we succeed as families, teams, and communities;

and as it happens, we fail that way as well. Owning one's mistakes is admirable, but responsibility for professional and socioeconomic disappointment could be more widely dispersed than most of our stories currently suggest. I want to emphasize that I don't just mean "you didn't build that" because teachers and communities helped you to succeed, which can frame collective success as a debit to individual merit. I mean you were never supposed to build that, that's not how life works, and congratulations to a group of people.

The downside to this approach, I realize, is that it can be spun into a privileged person's justification for privilege. Maybe you view Jeff's take on his last name and family resources as an excuse for exploiting advantage. But I think owning and celebrating help is preferable to minimizing it, explaining it away, or apologizing for it, which is what we frequently do now. What I like about the notion of collective success is that it promotes a sense that we can't really separate individual contributions from external variables, and leads to the sensible conclusion that we are fools to try. It invites people to pursue and enjoy good work and accomplishments while removing some of the individual stigma from people whom those elude.

2. I am talented.

The way we talk about talent is strange. In fall 2019 a Penn State football player named Jonathan Sutherland received a letter from an alum criticizing his "disgusting" dreadlocks. The letter caused a minor Internet kerfuffle because it was racist. One line that caught my attention was this: "I played all the sports in my younger days.... Loved the competition but never had the size or the talent to reach your level; though the desire was there!"[17]

The idea that desire or effort *should* be enough to determine success is a deeply rooted one, and actually sports is one of the only arenas in which "I wasn't talented enough" is a common and acceptable explanation for coming up short, plus it is a common feature of a racist worldview to attribute black athletes' success solely to physical talent. More often people describe effort as the predominant individual factor in success. We don't tell the surgeon or the electrician that they are there only because of their adept hands. It's like we want to imagine talent isn't a crucial factor right up until we pretend it's the only factor, depending on whom we wish to treat as deserving.

But of course talent and ability factor in hugely and complicatedly in many walks of life. Whether one's talent is innate or developed is an interesting question but not always a relevant one from a deservedness perspective. Both innate talents and many of those developed thanks to opportunity, particularly early in life, are unearned by American standards. Which is to say, "meritocracy" isn't unmeritocratic just when it is violated. It is unmeritocratic when it works. The most qualified person for a job didn't usually *earn* it in a deeper sense.

My suggestion is that we build on our conviction that talent is unearned, and embrace our sense that our role in developing it is indecipherable, in order to push back on the notion that "the right person for the job" can ever really deserve it. One way to do this would be to soften the taboo against citing one's own talent in explanations of success and tamp down our frequent emphasis on hard work. I regularly had to explicitly ask successful interviewees about talent to get them to acknowledge that it played a role for them. Talking up one's talent is considered boastful, while talking about how hard one worked is standard success story fare. But this is backwards, in a sense, because it's the story about how hard you worked that implies to listeners that *you earned this.*

While it is insulting to athletes to suggest that their success is due to physical talent alone, we would do well to acknowledge and emphasize the role of innate abilities in some of our other stories, and deny ourselves to some degree the profound credit of success due to effort. *Admit* that a big part of why you're a good salesperson is that you're naturally an extrovert who draws energy from talking to people. *Admit* that you managed to succeed in two different careers in large part because many things come easily to you, and that you probably didn't work that much harder than less successful people. There are only so many hours in the week, after all. Effort matters and is worthwhile. But it's not always the differentiator we make it out to be.

Americans want to "make something of themselves," argued Richard Sennett and Jonathan Cobb.[18] That's ultimately how professional success is linked up with dignity. Because we believe we can express our agency by using what we have—our time and mind and body—to succeed in the working world, many of us take success as proof of personal value. Perhaps we can take some of the pressure off the individual, and some of the weight off the results, by acknowledging that even if society got everything right (which it doesn't, and won't), this is not as much under our control as we'd like to think.

3. We are not *almost* or *sometimes* in a meritocracy. We are not in a meritocracy.

Back in chapter 1, I wrote about Carly Fiorina's "self-made" narrative and the backlash it engendered. Fiorina's father was a prominent attorney, critics observed. She probably had considerable help paying for Stanford. Her parents gave her a baby grand piano as a gift.

I'm sympathetic to these criticisms. But in framing objections to Fiorina this way, people frequently conceded the premise that a person *could* be self-made or achieve her station meritocratically. Arguments like this implicitly invite people to make a case that they, personally, earned their position.

Rather than criticize Fiorina for claiming to meet meritocratic criteria when she does not, someone might push back on the narrative by criticizing those criteria themselves. We might say that it's disrespectful of communal and familial efforts, not to mention out of step with reality, for people to claim to be self-made. We might move the goalposts from "you didn't do it" to "that's ridiculous." Fiorina should not be considered an avatar of meritocracy because *no one is*.

"*You specifically* don't deserve it and here's why" is a common form of attack even on people who don't claim to be self-made, and understandably so. For one thing, these attacks frequently rest on accurate observations about unmeritocratic processes, unequal opportunity, or unfair rewards. The world is rife with them. For another, these attacks are barbed, targeting as they do an individual's dignity, and meanness feels quite warranted when you are talking about, say, a CEO who grew up rich and now won't give his employees a raise, or a cocky Ivy League grad with a fancy job who condescends to his kid's teacher.

But this framing also encourages us to imagine that we live in a society that is a meritocracy with exceptions. A meritocracy except for class privilege. A meritocracy except for racism. A meritocracy except for nepotism. A meritocracy in some meaningful number of cases. This framing implies, somewhat strangely in my view, that the same institutions that, for example, disproportionately admit or hire white people rather than racial minorities are doing a good job of hiring the most meritorious white people, and that the minorities who manage to make it inside make it largely because of effort and ability and regardless of the questionable motives and judgment of the people in charge. A different kind of framing could suggest a different societal reality: that crucial structural factors set the boundaries of most of our paths, and our success and failure within those boundaries, as well as the rare cases in which people move outside of them, are attributable to a haphazard mix of circumstantial and individual variables, some of which have to do with merit but many of which do not.

It's not realistic to expect people to stop making "you specifically don't deserve it" arguments, especially about jerks. But I do think these could conceivably be complemented by more critiques that attack the meritocratic premise. For example, when the actresses Lori Loughlin and Felicity Huffman, along with a bunch of other rich people, were caught illegally manipulating the college admissions system to secure admission to selective colleges for their children, the premise could be attacked not by observing that more deserving students were cheated, nor even by arguing that *legal* legacy admissions also constitute a form of unmeritocratic reward, but by pointing out that admissions processes are inevitably, inherently flawed. We should lament the fact that the stakes of such a flawed process are so high in the first place.

4. Leave it to chance.

"People have a need to believe that their environment is a just and orderly place where people usually get what they deserve," according to Melvin Lerner's "just world" hypothesis.[19] Consequently, research has shown, people often find ways to blame victims for their suffering and develop weird rationalizations for why someone deserved an arbitrary reward. In one 1965 study, students who were told a fellow student had won a lottery believed the winner was a harder worker than others who had lost.

As you know by now, the people I interviewed did not generally describe a purely "just world" in their stories, and I don't think most people would—especially in a world with COVID-19. But I think we can detect people's discomfort with chaos, disorder, and randomness in these stories nonetheless. The way we identify actions we have taken that either explain or justify good or bad luck; the quasi-statistical logic we use that assumes luck evens out in the end—these are attempts to bring order to narratives of working lives. People are too observant to deny the existence of chance, but persuaded enough by (or committed enough to) the capacity of individuals to determine their own outcomes that we often talk our way out of accepting that luck can be decisive.

My suggestion here is simply to lean in more to the role of chance in stories. I heard comments like "I'm just along for the ride" or "It's mostly random" occasionally in my conversations but not often. Maybe something about these kinds of observations feels insufficiently explanatory in response to questions about how you got to where you are, the subtext of which can be read as "evaluate yourself." But it doesn't have to. A journalist profiling a politician, for example, doesn't necessarily need to figure out what makes him or her special. He could find the key explanatory circumstance rather than the key explanatory trait. Bernie Sanders "couldn't have come through those early face-offs with the 100 would-be Bernies back in Burlington without a high percentage of cold-bloodedness," declared a writer for *New York Magazine* explaining Sanders's rise in 2014.[20] Maybe. But maybe it's more important that Sanders was simply in the right place at the right time. Maybe he happened upon exactly the right mentor that some other Bernie never met.

Hell, maybe a better Bernie got hit by a bus. Random breaks don't actually even out in life, and more of our stories could treat circumstance as a star.

Ivanka Trump Has a Point

Taken together, I think the four storylines described in this chapter point toward a relationship with meritocracy that treats the concept not as an attainable ideal but as a flawed and unattainable guideline, with myriad exceptions and caveats. They accept that meritocracy is impossible to achieve and that the role of merit in any individual life is impossible to decipher.

You know who hints at this? Ivanka Trump: "Even though those who believe that my success is a result of nepotism might be right, they might also be wrong. Try as I may—and try as my critics may—there's just no way to measure the advantage I've gained from having the Trump name, just as there's no way to know if the person sitting across from you in a job interview or a negotiation is there on his or her own merits or with an assist of one kind or another."[21] We can, of course, identify and even weigh certain advantages and disadvantages, and in Trump's case, there is no chance she would be in her current position without nepotism. But there is something to what she is saying here. There is often no way to disentangle the role of merit in someone's life from so many other factors. The problem is that Trump draws the wrong conclusion from this observation. She concludes we should assume that people *do* deserve their position and get on with things. Instead, we should assume that they don't. Then a lot of new possibilities open up.

If we embrace the idea that "deserve's got nothing to do with it"—or at least not a whole lot, and even if it does, we'll never get to the bottom of it—we open a path toward a system that distributes rewards *and* opportunities more equally. Rewards for the obvious reason that there's less justification for a system where Jeff Bezos can amass $150 billion if he didn't earn it. Opportunities, meanwhile, would be easier to make closer to equal if the stakes of economic competition and social mobility were lower. Lower stakes would help to break Chris Hayes's "Iron Law of Meritocracy," wherein meritocracy's winners inevitably subvert equality of opportunity to make sure they and their children remain winners, both because more equally distributed rewards would leave elites with less power and fewer resources to manipulate outcomes, and because it would reduce their incentive to do so. Upper-middle-class people, for example, would have less reason to rig systems, hoard resources, or desperately exploit advantages if falling out of the upper middle class didn't mean precarious employment, uncertain access to health care, and a potentially profound loss of dignity.

From a policy perspective, advancing the notion that "deserve's got not much to do with it" begins with policies that seek not primarily to "level the playing field," as much contemporary liberal rhetoric emphasizes, but to improve the quality of life for as many as possible regardless of perceived individual deservedness. Universal health care is a policy proposal already in the national consciousness that meets these criteria. Other forms of government support that fit the bill include free school meals, free child care, and paid family leave, sick leave, and vacation. A universal basic income is worthy of consideration, and could be complemented by wage subsidies (paychecks to flatten out income inequality), direct cash support, and a jobs program, which would have the benefit of being in tune with the contemporary American understanding of deservedness as related to effort but not necessarily accurately reflected by the caprices of the market. These efforts to raise up the bottom of the income distribution could be paid for by measures that lower the top end, such as progressive taxation.

This kind of agenda would not preclude the pursuit of policies that explicitly seek to provide equality of opportunity, such as affirmative action and reforms to education, zoning, occupational licensing, etc. In fact, a "quality of life" agenda would probably level the playing field collaterally, by reducing the disparity in resources people could deploy in pursuit of success. It also would not obstruct measures that seek to right specific wrongs, such as reparations, the case for which is consistent with a broad acknowledgment that all of us operate under important social constraints. A "quality of life" agenda would simply refuse to treat success as a prerequisite for comfort, and it would proceed on the assumption that even with a more level playing field, we won't be living in a meritocracy.

Most of these proposals will be familiar to people who follow American politics, which is part of why I've dedicated less than one page of this book to them. What I hope I'm offering is a different justification for such a program. As Jhumpa Bhattacharya and Anne Price have written for the Economic Security Project, economic reforms aimed at inequity "could fail immensely without first tackling narrative," which helps establish our expectations and preferences for how a society should work.[22] The narrative tweaks I propose here are not fixes to get us closer to meritocracy. They are fixes to get us away from the delusion that we can be a meritocracy.

Speaking of delusions, I am not so deluded as to think the argument that "deserve's got not much to do with it" would appeal to everyone. Some Americans, particularly highly successful ones, will remain committed to the idea that we are *close enough* to a meritocracy to justify their high status. Conservatives ideologically opposed to government interference in the market won't be interested in redistributive policies framed as a corrective to meritocracy, because their opposition to such policies was not predicated on deservedness in the first place. Plenty of people will remain committed to the belief that poverty in America is caused by moral failings. In many cases, this belief will still be motivated by racism. Still, casting doubt on the meritocratic premise by emphasizing the inevitability of unfairness and arbitrariness, and the inability of the individual to overcome them in many cases, would provide a different kind of counterweight to the self-made stories and meritocratic themes that permeate our culture—a counterweight that weakens the link between success in one's working life and personal dignity.

"Deserve's got not much to do with it" does not mean personal responsibility doesn't matter (taking responsibility for one's actions shouldn't be linked to reward anyway) or that effort is pointless; trying should still be understood as useful, and is certainly a better plan than *not* trying. It just means that the market is capricious and life is complex in ways we can't control, and so the realization of "true" meritocracy does not make sense as a priority.

We were starting to hear more arguments along these lines in mainstream American culture even before 2020 dawned. I was particularly struck by a Nike ad featuring LeBron James, in which James begins by saying:

> We always hear about an athlete's humble beginnings.
> How they emerged from poverty or tragedy to beat the odds.
> They're supposed to be the stories of determination that capture the American dream.
> They're supposed to be stories to let you know these people are special.

Then James says:

> But you know what would be really special?
> If there were no more humble beginnings.

This is a Nike commercial, designed to sell clothing. But it was surprising to me, after reading so many stories of success, to hear a story that turns a humble roots narrative on its head, rejecting the premise that humble roots are something to be celebrated because someone overcame them through merit, and instead lamenting them because poverty and tragedy are bad. This is a story that deprioritizes meritocracy in favor of other values. It doesn't concern itself, first and foremost, with what is earned or deserved in the American economy.

The cultural current this represents was beginning to move before COVID-19 hit and Black Lives Matter protests took off. Now we have even more profound evidence that we are not the authors of our own fates and, more important, that figuring out whether someone comes close just isn't a terribly important question. We should embrace that reality rather than explain it away.

I Didn't Earn This

A few readers of drafts of this book suggested that I start off by explaining my own career path and exploring the question of my own merit, to give readers context and as a sort of disclosure. I resisted because I didn't want you to think (catch on?) that I was writing a book about "we" "Americans" that was really all about my own hang-ups.

Now, however, I will note that the premise of meritocracy has influenced my life profoundly. Both of my parents come from immigrant families who bought in to the promise of hard work and educational attainment as steps on a ladder toward upper-middle-class security and opportunity. Their success opened pathways for their children. I attended Hunter College High School, a school that sends a ridiculous percentage of its graduates on to prestigious universities and has an absurd list of prominent alumni. (I was there at the same time as *Hamilton* creator Lin-Manuel Miranda and played on the basketball team with MSNBC host Chris Hayes, who wrote *Twilight of the Elites: America after Meritocracy.*) Then I went to a bunch of fancy-pants schools for my undergraduate and graduate degrees.

That is a lot of upward trajectory and educational opportunity. (It's probably not a coincidence that I am the second person from my era at Hunter to write a book about meritocracy. Very probably the less successful book about meritocracy, which is funny I guess.) It should be no surprise, then, that I spent a lot of time in my twenties and thirties thinking about whether I had gone far enough or earned what I had. I think I tried to figure out the criteria for success and failure in America in part just so I could decide once and for all whether I met them.

The moments in my interviews that stuck with me most, though, were the rare ones when interviewees rejected my assumptions about the importance of merit. When Pam said, "I feel like we go overboard with the 'I earned' and 'I deserved'"; when Erica said, "No one earns what they get," right after saying "Everyone deserves to get what they want"; when Joe said that he was only worried about whether he worked hard because the rest was out of his control; when Josh said that he didn't intend to work hard unless he cared about the work; when Grace, a medical student from a privileged background, said that she had earned nothing, and then looked at me and said with conviction, "I'm proud of what I've done so far with my life."

These kinds of comments go further than simply saying "I feel blessed," which Americans say a lot. They reject the basic logic of trying to link dignity to socioeconomic outcomes.

I get that there is something of a trick question quality to what I've done here. "Did you earn it?" I asked people, only to turn around and say, "Wrong! The correct answer was 'I don't like the question.'" But I think it's safe to say that most Americans accept the premise that meritocracy is possible and important. For me, the willingness of a few interviewees to push back on this premise felt liberating.

Maybe this perspective is particularly appealing to me because of all the time I've spent in elite educational institutions, where meritocratic achievement is a preoccupation. But the idea that you can and should rise and fall according to efforts and abilities doesn't only matter in admissions offices. It affects the salesman trying to hit his numbers, the nurse seeking a promotion, the contractor whose competitor puts him out of business. My sense is that it would be socially beneficial if more people felt invited—if they found the option on the cultural menu—to tell a story in which deserve's got not much to do with it, and they are not solely responsible for their outcomes.

People like Darrell the ex-con, Susan the office manager, Anita who works in a hotel kitchen, and Mark who works at a grocery store, who feel like disappointments and point a finger at themselves, stand to benefit from a story in which they shoulder less blame.

People like Laura the therapy student and Erica the EMT trainee, who feel guilty about and pressured by their advantages, stand to benefit from a story in which they carry less expectation.

People like Jon the future mayor, Paul who works for his dad, and Nick the corporate attorney, who self-consciously stretch to justify their successes, stand to benefit from a story that puts less emphasis on the question of whether they've earned their position.

So do people like Linda the dairy farmer and Philip Mitchell, who see the structural forces working against them and feel vexed by the distance between how their lives work and how their lives are supposed to work.

The main category of people I can think of who might strenuously object to the argument that "deserve's got not much to do with it" are people deeply invested in telling self-made stories, and frankly, those people get plenty of affirmation from American culture. They'll be okay.

Americans already generally view success and failure in our working lives as the product of a complex combination of effort, ability, social structures, and luck. But we nevertheless mostly explain individual lives through stories that assume people *can* earn or deserve their outcomes through merit, and we aim to figure out if they have. The idea that life doesn't work this way, and likely never will, could help us tell stories that build on our more nuanced perception of the world around us. It could help a lot of people feel better about what they've done with their lives. It could help justify a political agenda that seeks to provide people a better life, directly and immediately. Plus, it's true.

Acknowledgments

I cannot thank the people I interviewed for this book by name, but they spoke with me because they are the type of people who help other people out, and I am in their debt. Several people helped me to recruit interviewees, and their names I can share: Greg Anderson, James Beale, Molly Eichel, Jeff Milman, Sheree Moore, Juliana Reyes, Alex Shorb, Maurice Walls, Andrew Zitcer. Thank you all.

For their help in conceiving and executing this project, I want to thank Michael Delli Carpini, Kathleen Hall Jamieson, Joseph Turow, and Barbie Zelizer from the Annenberg School for Communication at the University of Pennsylvania. Jeff Lane, Nancy Morris, Doug Porpora, and Keeanga-Yamahtta Taylor provided generous guidance as well. For insightful reads of drafts, enthusiastic support, and valued friendship, I thank James Beale, Jason England, Michael Budabin McQuown, and Sara Primo—and Jason also for a running text conversation about meritocracy, politics, and other things that make us angry.

My colleagues in Media and Communications Studies at Ursinus College have been extremely kind and supportive as I've finished this book over my first two years at the school. Lynne Edwards, Jennifer Fleeger, Sheryl Goodman, Alice Leppert, Tony Nadler, and Louise Woodstock—thank you.

Throughout this process, Mike Ambrogi Primo has kindly listened to me complain on many commutes and a few runs. The members of Mt. Airy Dadball have patiently allowed me to shoot my way out of quite a few slumps, and Brendan Hart, Chris Malanga, and Kayvon Nikoo have added valuable analysis and mockery.

My parents, Gabe and Ethel Taussig, have supported me in everything I have done or tried to do in my life. I have also been blessed with kind in-laws in Paul Koehler and Luray Gross, and a spectacular sister in Dana Taussig. My children, Sam, Leo, and Hana Taussig, are all so wonderful in so many ways, and I want to thank them for it. I don't know where I'd be without Chelsea.

Appendix A
Personal Merit Narrative Interview Protocol

This is the general guideline that I used for interviews. Interviews took place in 2016 and 2017.

The purpose of this project is to explore how people think they got to where they are and how important these issues are to them. I'm going to ask you some questions about your own life. If you are uncomfortable with a question, please tell me and we can skip the question or stop the interview.

1. Please tell me about yourself—where you come from, where you are now, and how you got here.
2. Do you feel like a success?
3. Why did your successes and/or failures happen?
4. In what ways have you been advantaged in life? In what ways have you been disadvantaged?
5. Do you think that most people born into your circumstances would end up with a similar life to yours?
6. Do you think your life could have gone differently? What is another path you can imagine for yourself? What would have had to change for you to end up there?
7. Do you think you've earned what you have/where you are?
8. One of the important ideas about America is that it is supposed to be a meritocracy, meaning people are supposed to end up

about where they deserve to be, or get what they earn, on the basis of their efforts and abilities. Has your life worked that way?

9. Do you think America more broadly is working as a meritocracy? When you look at the world around you, do you see people ending up about where they deserve to be?

10. What separates the people who have done well from the people who have not?

11. What are/were your thoughts on the 2016 election?

12. Do you think Donald Trump deserves to be in his position?

13. Do you think Hillary Clinton deserves to be in her position?

Appendix B

Interviewee Demographics

TABLE 1

Occupation	Age	Race	Gender
Fighting for SSI	49	Black	M
Contracting	46	Black	M
Office manager	42	Black	M
Retired, previously sales	66	Mixed	M
Afterschool program counselor	26	White	F
Afterschool program counselor	21	Black	M
EMT trainee	24	Black	F
Clergy	Senior	Black	M
Catering/promotions/unemployed	52	Black	M
Retired military, illustrator/unemployed	57	Black	M
Retired social worker	76	Black/ Latinx	F
Computer technician	28	Black	M
Hotel kitchen worker	37	Black	F
Grocery store employee	25	Black	M
Social worker	34	Black	F
Adult educator	61	Black	F
Computer technician	25	Black	M

(*continued*)

TABLE 1 (*continued*)

Occupation	Age	Race	Gender
Pharmacist/EMT trainee	28	White	M
Police officer	59	Black	M
Drug dealer	27	White	F
Retired farmer/agriculture educator	77	White	F
Retired machinist/vocational school teacher	86	White	M
Retired planner	81	White	M
Retired state employee	60s	White	M
Retail store manager	57	White	M
Teacher	35	Black	F
Unemployed	31	Black	F
Collects disability	59	Black	M
State employee	62	Black/Latinx	F
Graduate student	28	White	M
Investor/researcher	50	White	M
Assistant manager, former draftsman	34	White	M
Dairy farmer	60s	White	F
Contractor	69	White	M
Corporate lawyer	28	White	M
Medical student	26	Black	F
Probation officer	31	Black	F
Office manager	53	White	F
Grocery store employee	44	White	M
Retail (former road crew worker)	56	White	M
Massage therapist	30s	White	F
Project manager for a general contractor	Middle-aged	White	M
Therapy student	27	White	F
CEO	56	Middle Eastern	M
Executive director at a nonprofit	38	White	M

Occupation	Age	Race	Gender
Partner in family business	32	White	M
Artist	39	Asian	M
State government employee/former lawyer	41	Asian	F
Fireman	52	White	M
Tech startup CEO	31	White	F
CFO	37	White	F
Financial adviser	40	White	M
Housewife	Middle-aged	White	F
Retired military intelligence	70	White	M
Consultant/finance	59	White	M
State house staffer	21	White	M
Political operative and line cook	25	White	M
Retired executive director at a nonprofit	76	White	M
Retired grocery store manager	88	White	M
Retired social worker	59	Black	F

Notes

Introduction

1. Sheryl Sandberg, *Lean In* (New York: Random House, 2013), 63.

2. "Fox's Rove: Clinton 'Has Been Successful in Life When She Has Made Herself a Victim,'" Media Matters for America, May 16, 2016, https://www.me diamatters.org/video/2016/05/16/foxs-rove-clinton-has-been-successful-life-when-she-has-made-herself-victim/210452.

3. Andrew Dugan and Frank Newport, "In U.S., Fewer Believe 'Plenty of Opportunity' to Get Ahead," Gallup, October 25, 2013, http://www.gallup.com/poll/165584/fewer-believe-plenty-opportunity-ahead.aspx; Ruth Igielnik, "70% of Americans Say U.S. Economic System Unfairly Favors the Powerful," Pew Research Center, January 9, 2020, https://www.pewresearch.org/fact-tank/2020/01/09/70-of-americans-say-u-s-economic-system-unfairly-favors-the-powerful/.

4. Eugene Kiely, "'You Didn't Build That,' Uncut and Unedited," *Factcheck.org*, July 23, 2012, https://www.factcheck.org/2012/07/you-didnt-build-that-uncut-and-unedited/.

5. David Corn, "Secret Video: Romney Tells Millionaire Donors What He Really Thinks of Obama Voters," *Mother Jones*, September 17, 2012, https://www.motherjones.com/politics/2012/09/secret-video-romney-private-fundraiser/.

6. Joseph F. Kett, *Merit: The History of a Founding Ideal from the American Revolution to the Twenty-First Century* (Ithaca: Cornell University Press, 2012).

7. Jonathan F. Anderson, "The Gospel According to Merit: From Virtue to Rationality to Production," *International Journal of Organization Theory and Behavior* 16, no. 4 (2013): 449.

8. Amartya Sen, "Merit and Justice," in *Meritocracy and Economic Inequality*, ed. Kenneth Arrow, Samuel Bowles, and Steven N. Durlauf (Princeton: Princeton University Press, 2000), 5–16.

9. John Carson, *The Measure of Merit: Talents, Intelligence, and Inequality in the French and American Republics, 1750–1940* (Princeton: Princeton University Press, 2007), 5.

10. Richard Arneson, "Four Conceptions of Equal Opportunity," *Economic Journal* 128, no. 612 (2018): F152–73.

11. Michael Dunlop Young, *The Rise of the Meritocracy, 1870–2033: The New Elite of Our Social Revolution* (1958, New York: Random House, 1959).

12. Christopher Hayes, *Twilight of the Elites: America after Meritocracy* (New York: Broadway Books, 2013).

13. Robert K. Miller and Stephen J. McNamee, *The Meritocracy Myth* (Lanham, MD: Rowman & Littlefield, 2013).

14. Miller and McNamee, *The Meritocracy Myth*, 2.

15. Hayes, *Twilight of the Elites*.

16. Joan Huber and William Humbert Form, *Income and Ideology: An Analysis of the American Political Formula* (New York: Free Press, 1973), 4.

17. Miller and McNamee, *The Meritocracy Myth*; Jennifer Hochschild, *Facing Up to the American Dream: Race, Class, and the Soul of the Nation* (Princeton: Princeton University Press, 1996).

18. James R. Kluegel and Eliot R. Smith, *Beliefs about Inequality: Americans' Views of What Is and What Ought to Be* (Chicago: Aldine, 1986); Jeremy Reynolds and He Xian, "Perceptions of Meritocracy in the Land of Opportunity," *Research in Social Stratification and Mobility* 36 (2014): 121–37.

19. Eugene Kiely, "'You Didn't Build That,' Uncut and Unedited."

20. Richard Sennett and Jonathan Cobb, *The Hidden Injuries of Class* (New York: Alfred A. Knopf, 1972), 245.

21. Michele Lamont, *Money, Morals, and Manners: The Culture of the French and the American Upper-Middle Class* (Chicago: University of Chicago Press, 1992); Shamus Khan, *Privilege: The Making of an Adolescent Elite at St. Paul's School* (Princeton: Princeton University Press, 2011).

22. Katherine S. Newman, *Falling from Grace: The Experience of Downward Mobility in the American Middle Class* (New York: Free Press, 1988).

23. Sennett and Cobb, *The Hidden Injuries of Class*, 96.

24. Mark Leibovich, "The Aria of Chris Matthews," *New York Times Magazine*, April 13, 2008, https://www.nytimes.com/2008/04/13/magazine/13matthews-t.html.

25. See Nikole Hannah-Jones, "What is Owed," *New York Times Magazine*, June 30, 2020, https://www.nytimes.com/interactive/2020/06/24/magazine/reparations-slavery.html; Isabel Wilkerson, "America's Enduring Caste System," *New York Times Magazine*, July 1, 2020, https://www.nytimes.com/2020/07/01/magazine/isabel-wilkerson-caste.html.

26. Karen Sternheimer, *Celebrity Culture and the American Dream: Stardom and Social Mobility* (New York: Routledge, 2011).

27. Kluegel and Smith, *Beliefs about Inequality*, 1.

28. Walter R. Fisher, "Narration as a Human Communication Paradigm: The Case of Public Moral Argument," *Communications Monographs* 51, no. 1 (1984): 1–22.

29. Charlotte Linde, *Life Stories: The Creation of Coherence* (New York: Oxford University Press, 1993).

30. Fisher, "Narration as a Human Communication Paradigm," 7.

31. Dan P. McAdams, "Personal Narratives and the Life Story," in *Handbook of Personality: Theory and Research*, ed. Oliver P. John and Lawrence A. Pervin (New York: Guilford Press, 1999), 478.

32. Catherine K. Riessman, *Narrative Analysis* (Newbury Park, CA: Sage Publications, 1993).

33. Helen Andrews, "The New Ruling Class," *Hedgehog Review* 18, no. 2 (2016), https://hedgehogreview.com/issues/meritocracy-and-its-discontents/articles/the-new-ruling-class.

34. Sacvan Bercovitch, *The Rites of Assent: Transformations in the Symbolic Construction of America* (New York: Routledge, 1993), 366.

1. American Idols

1. Michelle Ye Hee Lee, "Carly Fiorina's 'Secretary to CEO' Career Trajectory," *Washington Post*, September 25, 2015, https://www.washingtonpost.com/news/fact-checker/wp/2015/09/25/carly-fiorinas-bogus-secretary-to-ceo-career-trajectory-fact-checker-biography/?utm_term=.c188cc491ea9.

2. John Sexton, "Howard Kurtz: Washington Post's Take on Carly Fiorina a 'Misfire,'" Breitbart, September 28, 2015, https://www.breitbart.com/politics/2015/09/28/howard-kurtz-washington-posts-take-carly-fiorina-misfire/.

3. Lee, "Carly Fiorina's 'Secretary to CEO' Career Trajectory."

4. Kevin Drum, "Carly's Ex Doesn't Think Much of Her Chances," *Mother Jones*, September 22, 2015, https://www.motherjones.com/kevin-drum/2015/09/quote-day-carlys-ex-doesnt-think-much-her-chances/.

5. Claire Sparks, comment on Michelle Ye Hee Lee, "Carly Fiorina's 'Secretary to CEO' Career Trajectory," *Washington Post*, September 25, 2015, https://www.washingtonpost.com/news/fact-checker/wp/2015/09/25/carly-fiorinas-bogus-secretary-to-ceo-career-trajectory-fact-checker-biography/?utm_term=.c188cc491ea9.

6. BurbankBob, comment on Lee, "Carly Fiorina's 'Secretary to CEO' Career Trajectory"; Lee Pelletier, comment on Lee, "Carly Fiorina's 'Secretary to CEO' Career Trajectory."

7. Brian Stewart (@BrianStewartOH), Twitter post, September 25, 2015, https://twitter.com/BrianStewartOH/status/647401767991439360.

8. Tom Blumer, "WashPost's 'Fact Checker' Goes Full Politifact over Fiorina's 'Secretary to CEO' Bio," NewsBusters, September 29, 2015, https://www.news busters.org/blogs/nb/tom-blumer/2015/09/29/washposts-fact-checker-goes-full-politifact-over-fiorinas-secretary.

9. Leo Lowenthal, "The Triumph of Mass Idols," in *Literature and Mass Culture* (1944; New York: Routledge, 1984), 207.

10. Brooke E. Duffy and Jefferson Pooley, "Idols of Promotion: The Triumph of Self-Branding in an Age of Precarity," *Journal of Communication* 69, no. 1 (2017): 26–48.

11. Emmett Winn, "Moralizing Upward Mobility: Investigating the Myth of Class Mobility in *Working Girl*," *Southern Journal of Communication* 66, no. 1 (2000): 40–51; Russell Meeuf, "The Nonnormative Celebrity Body and the Meritocracy of the Star System: Constructing Peter Dinklage in Entertainment Journalism," *Journal of Communication Inquiry* 38, no. 3 (2014): 204–22.

12. Matt Stahl, "A Moment Like This: *American Idol* and Narratives of Meritocracy," in *Bad Music: The Music We Love to Hate*, ed. Christopher J. Washburne and Maiken Derno (New York: Routledge, 2004), 212–32.

13. Sut Jhally and Justin Lewis, *Enlightened Racism: The Cosby Show, Audiences, and the Myth of the American Dream* (New York: Routledge, 1992); Mary M. Dalton and Laura R. Linder, "1980s Normalizing Meritocracy: The Facts of Life and Head of the Class," *Counterpoints*, no. 320 (2008): 75–100.

14. Julian Jefferies, "Do Undocumented Students Play by the Rules? Meritocracy in the Media," *Critical Inquiry in Language Studies* 6, no. 1–2 (2009): 15–38.

15. Karen Sternheimer, *Celebrity Culture and the American Dream: Stardom and Social Mobility* (New York: Routledge, 2011), 6.

16. Joanne Morreale, *The Presidential Campaign Film: A Critical History* (Westport, CT: Praeger Publishers, 1993), 8.

17. Brian Miller and Mike Lapham, *The Self-Made Myth: And the Truth about How Government Helps Individuals and Businesses Succeed* (San Francisco: Berrett-Koehler Publishers, 2012), 2.

18. Michael Serazio, "Why Sports Should Be More Political," *Bloomberg View*, January 12, 2017, https://www.bloomberg.com/view/articles/2017-01-12/why-sports-should-be-more-political.

19. Sean Crosson, "From Babe Ruth to Michael Jordan: Affirming the American Dream via the Sports/Film Star," *Kinema* 42, no. 79 (2014): 1–14, https://openjournals.uwaterloo.ca/index.php/kinema/article/view/1299/1687.

20. Sternheimer, *Celebrity Culture and the American Dream*.

21. Sternheimer, *Celebrity Culture and the American Dream*, 3.

22. Crosson, "From Babe Ruth to Michael Jordan," 7.

23. Richard Giulianotti, *Football: A Sociology of the Global Game* (Cambridge: Polity, 1999), 118–19.

24. Susan Birrell, "Racial Relations Theories and Sport: Suggestions for a More Critical Analysis," *Sociology of Sport Journal* 6, no. 3 (1989): 213.

25. Sternheimer, *Celebrity Culture and the American Dream*, 17.

26. Kathleen Hall Jamieson, *Packaging the Presidency* (New York: Oxford University Press, 1984).

27. Howard Fineman, "And Now, Log Cabin Chic," *Newsweek*, November 30, 1987, Nexis Uni.

28. Howard Fineman, "You Owe It to Me Now," *Newsweek*, January 18, 1988, Nexis Uni.

29. Sidney Blumenthal, "The Candidate from Kansas; Robert Dole, the Insider from the Outside, Aiming for the White House," *Washington Post*, November 9, 1987, Nexis Uni.

30. Frank Clifford, "Conservatives Attack Bush, Dole in Lively Debate," *Los Angeles Times*, January 17, 1988, https://www.latimes.com/archives/la-xpm-1988-01-17-mn-36770-story.html.

31. Blumenthal, "The Candidate from Kansas."

32. George H. W. Bush, "Address Accepting the Republican Presidential Nomination at the Republican National Convention in New Orleans," The American Presidency Project, https://www.presidency.ucsb.edu/documents/address-accepting-the-presidential-nomination-the-republican-national-convention-new.

33. Joyce Purnick and Michael Oreskes, "Jesse Jackson Aims for the Mainstream," *New York Times Magazine*, November 29, 1987, Nexis Uni.

34. James N. Baker, "A Compendium of Troubling Issues–Past and Present," *Newsweek*, April 11, 1988, Nexis Uni.

35. Purnick and Oreskes, "Jesse Jackson Aims for the Mainstream."

36. Gail Sheehy, "Jackson's Lifelong Quest for Legitimacy," *Chicago Tribune*, June 12, 1988, http://articles.chicagotribune.com/1988-06-12/features/8801070166_1_jesse-noah-robinson-black.

37. Purnick and Oreskes, "Jesse Jackson Aims for the Mainstream."

38. Purnick and Oreskes, "Jesse Jackson Aims for the Mainstream."

39. Larry Martz, Howard Fineman, Sylvester Monroe, Eleanor Clift, and Andrew Murr, "The Power Broker," *Newsweek*, March 21, 1988, Nexis Uni.

40. Martz et al., "The Power Broker"; Jonathan Alter, "Political Sin and Forgiveness," *Newsweek*, April 25, 1988, Nexis Uni; Baker, "A Compendium of Troubling Issues"; Walter Shapiro, "Taking Jesse Seriously." *Time*, April 11, 1988, http://content.time.com/time/magazine/article/0,9171,967157,00.html.

41. Shapiro, "Taking Jesse Seriously."

42. George Will, "Politics as Autobiography, *Washington Post*, July 20, 1988, Nexis Uni.

43. David Broder, "Dukakis' Lessons of Defeat, Victory, and Growth," *Washington Post*, June 29, 1987, Nexis Uni.

44. Michael Boskin, "Dukakis' 'Miracle' Only a Mirage," *Los Angeles Times*, August 21, 1988, http://articles.latimes.com/1988-08-21/business/fi-1266_1_massachusetts-miracle.

45. "Candidate Profile: Jeb Bush," *The Onion*, June 15, 2015, http://www.theonion.com/graphic/candidate-profile-jeb-bush-50664.

46. Margaret Talbot, "The Populist Prophet," *The New Yorker*, October 12, 2015, https://www.newyorker.com/magazine/2015/10/12/the-populist-prophet.

47. "This May Be the Most Dangerous Thing Donald Trump Believes," *Huffington Post*, http://www.huffingtonpost.com/entry/donald-trump-genes-eugenics_us_58ffd428e4b0af6d71898737.

48. Jane Mayer, "Donald Trump's Ghostwriter Tells All," *The New Yorker*, July 25, 2016, https://www.newyorker.com/magazine/2016/07/25/donald-trumps-ghostwriter-tells-all.

49. "Fox's Rove: Clinton 'Has Been Successful in Life When She Has Made Herself a Victim,'" Media Matters, May 16, 2016, https://www.mediamatters.org/video/2016/05/16/foxs-rove-clinton-has-been-successful-life-when-she-has-made-herself-victim/210452.

50. "Republican Candidates Debate in Simi Valley, California," The American Presidency Project, https://www.presidency.ucsb.edu/documents/republican-candidates-debate-simi-valley-california-0.

51. Ivanka Trump, *The Trump Card: Playing to Win in Work and Life* (New York: Simon and Schuster, 2009), 1–2.

52. Miller and Lapham, *The Self-Made Myth*, 2.

53. Lee Iacocca and William Novak, *Iacocca: An Autobiography* (New York: Bantam, 1984), 57.

54. Biz Stone, *Things a Little Bird Told Me* (New York: Pan Macmillan, 2014), xv.

55. Mary Kay Ash, *Mary Kay: Miracles Happen* (1981; New York: HarperCollins, 1994), 12.

56. Iacocca and Novak, *Iacocca*, 57.

57. Ash, *Mary Kay*, 12.

58. Iacocca and Novak, *Iacocca*, 57.

59. Ash, *Mary Kay*, 9, 120.

60. Sheryl Sandberg, *Lean In: Women, Work, and the Will to Lead* (New York: Random House, 2013), 10–11.

61. Rick Telander, "Ready . . . Set . . . Levitate!" *Sports Illustrated*, November 17, 1986, https://vault.si.com/vault/1986/11/17/readysetlevitate.

62. Sam Miller, "The Phenom," ESPN.com, September 20, 2012, http://www.espn.com/mlb/story/_/id/8392192/los-angeles-angels-centerfielder-mike-trout-phenom-last-espn-magazine.

63. Peter Gammons, "Mattingly Ends His Year Fittingly," *Sports Illustrated*, October 13, 1986, https://www.si.com/vault/1986/10/13/114161/mattingly-ends-his-year-fittingly-don-mattingly-couldnt-catch-wade-boggs-in-the-batting-race-but-he-demonstrated-why-hes-now-accepted-as-the-best-in-the-game.

64. William Nack, "Ready to Soar to the Very Top," *Sports Illustrated*, January 6, 1986, https://www.si.com/vault/1986/01/06/640815/ready-to-soar-to-the-very-top.

65. John Papanek, "Gifts That God Didn't Give," *Sports Illustrated*, November 9, 1981, https://www.si.com/vault/1981/11/09/826097/gifts-that-god-didnt-give-larry-bird-was-blessed-with-his-height-but-lots-of-work-made-him-the-nbas-most-complete-player-since-oscar-robertson.

66. Jack McCallum, "As Nearly Perfect as You Can Get," *Sports Illustrated*, March 3, 1986, https://www.si.com/vault/1986/03/03/628910/as-nearly-perfect-as-you-can-get.

67. Eugenio Mercurio and Vincent F. Filak, "Roughing the Passer: The Framing of Black and White Quarterbacks Prior to the NFL Draft," *Howard Journal of Communications* 21, no. 1 (2010): 56–71.

68. Philip Hersh, "Chasing Katie Ledecky," espnW, August 4, 2016, http://www.espn.com/espn/feature/story/_/page/espnw-ledecky160804/what-makes-olympic-swimmer-katie-ledecky-remarkable.

69. Miller, "The Phenom."

70. Papanek, "Gifts That God Didn't Give."

71. Joe Morgenstern, "Worldbeater: Olympic Athlete Jackie Joyner-Kersee," *New York Times Magazine*, July 31, 1988, http://www.nytimes.com/1988/07/31/magazine/worldbeater-olympic-athlete-jackie-joyner-kersee.html?pagewanted=all.

72. Phil Elderkin, "Many Reasons for Don Mattingly's Big Year," *Christian Science Monitor*, September 17, 1984, https://www.csmonitor.com/1984/0917/091704.html.

73. Chris Jones, "Conor McGregor Doesn't Believe in Death," *Esquire*, April 15, 2015, http://www.esquire.com/sports/interviews/a34377/conor-mcgregor-interview-0515/.

74. David Fleming, "Stephen Curry: The Full Circle," *ESPN The Magazine*, April 23, 2015, http://www.espn.com/espn/feature/story/_/id/12728744/how-golden-state-warriors-stephen-curry-became-nba-best-point-guard.

75. Jones, "Conor McGregor Doesn't Believe in Death."

76. Daniel Riley, "The MVP in Mom's Basement," *GQ*, March 27, 2013, https://www.gq.com/story/mlb-mike-trout-rookie-of-year.

77. Hersh, "Chasing Katie Ledecky."

78. Jason Gay, "The Incomparable Serena Williams," *WSJ Magazine*, July–August 2016, https://www.wsj.com/articles/the-incomparable-serena-williams-1466362801.

79. S. L. Price, "Serena Williams Is *Sports Illustrated*'s 2015 Sportsperson of the Year," *Sports Illustrated*, December 14, 2015, https://www.si.com/sportsperson/2015/12/14/serena-williams-si-sportsperson-year.

80. Papanek, "Gifts That God Didn't Give."

81. Michael Stone, "Strokes of Genius," *New York Magazine*, August 31, 1987, 48.

82. Gay, "The Incomparable Serena Williams."

83. Jones, "Conor McGregor Doesn't Believe in Death."

84. Morgenstern, "Worldbeater."

85. Murray Chass, "Every Pitcher's Nightmare; Why Don Mattingly is Baseball's Best Hitter," *New York Times*, April 3, 1988, http://www.nytimes.com/1988/04/03/magazine/every-pitcher-s-nightmare-why-don-mattingly-is-baseball-s-best-hitter.html?pagewanted=all.

86. Tom Callahan, "Boxing's Allure: From the Heart of a Primal Passion Comes the Terror of Mike Tyson," *Time*, June 27, 1988, 66–71, Factiva.

87. Stone, "Strokes of Genius," 50.

88. Howie Kahn, "Serena Williams, Wonder Woman, Is Our September Cover Star," *Self*, August 1, 2016, https://www.self.com/story/serena-williams-september-cover-interview.

2. Head Starts and Handicaps

1. Robert L. Simon, "Equality, Merit, and the Determination of Our Gifts," *Social Research* 41, no. 3 (1974): 497.

2. Richard Sennett and Jonathan Cobb, *The Hidden Injuries of Class* (New York: Alfred A. Knopf, 1972), 250.

3. Jennifer M. Silva, *Coming Up Short: Working-Class Adulthood in an Age of Uncertainty* (New York: Oxford University Press, 2013), 4.

4. James R. Kluegel and Eliot R. Smith, *Beliefs about Inequality: Americans' Views of What Is and What Ought to Be* (Chicago: Aldine, 1986).

5. Phoebe Maltz Bovy, *The Perils of Privilege* (New York: St. Martin's Press, 2017).

6. See, e.g., R. Patrick Solomona, John P. Portelli, Beverly-Jean Daniel, and Arlene Campbell, "The Discourse of Denial: How White Teacher Candidates Construct Race, Racism, and 'White Privilege,'" *Race Ethnicity and Education* 8, no. 2 (2005): 147–69; Eric D. Knowles and Brian S. Lowery, "Meritocracy, Self-Concerns, and Whites' Denial of Racial Inequity," *Self and Identity* 11, no. 2 (2012): 202–22.

7. Knowles and Lowery, "Meritocracy, Self-Concerns, and Whites' Denial of Racial Inequity," 2.

8. Don Gonyea, "Majority of White Americans Say They Believe Whites Face Discrimination," NPR, October 24, 2017, https://www.npr.org/2017/10/24/559604836/majority-of-white-americans-think-theyre-discriminated-against.

9. Janny Scott and David Leonhardt, "Shadowy Lines That Still Divide," *New York Times*, May 15, 2005, https://www.nytimes.com/2005/05/15/us/class/shadowy-lines-that-still-divide.html.

3. Me, Myself, and I

1. Joan Didion, *Slouching towards Bethlehem* (New York: Macmillan, 1990), 72.

2. Eliza Shapiro, "Only 7 Black Students Got into Stuyvesant, New York's Most Selective High School, Out of 895 Spots," *New York Times*, March 18, 2019, https://www.nytimes.com/2019/03/18/nyregion/black-students-nyc-high-schools.html.

3. Bill de Blasio, "Our Specialized Schools Have a Diversity Problem. Let's Fix It," *Chalkbeat*, June 2, 2018, https://chalkbeat.org/posts/ny/2018/06/02/mayor-bill-de-blasio-new-york-city-will-push-for-admissions-changes-at-elite-and-segregated-specialized-high-schools/.

4. Jerome Karabel, *The Chosen: The Hidden History of Admission and Exclusion at Harvard, Yale, and Princeton* (Boston: Houghton Mifflin Harcourt, 2006).

5. Nicholas Lemann, *The Big Test: The Secret History of the American Meritocracy* (New York: Macmillan, 2000).

6. Lisa Stampnitzky, "How Does 'Culture' Become 'Capital'? Cultural and Institutional Struggles over 'Character and Personality' at Harvard," *Sociological Perspectives* 49, no. 4 (2006): 472, 475.

7. Richard T. Longoria, "Meritocracy and Americans' Views on Distributive Justice" (PhD diss., University of Maryland, 2007), 3.

8. Robert K. Miller and Stephen J. McNamee, *The Meritocracy Myth* (Lanham, MD: Rowman & Littlefield, 2013).

9. Angela Duckworth, *Grit: The Power of Passion and Perseverance* (New York: Scribner, 2016).

10. Jonathan Mijs, "Earning Rent with Your Talent: Modern-Day Inequality Rests on the Power to Define, Transfer and Institutionalize Talent," *Educational Philosophy and Theory* (2018), doi: 10.1080/00131857.2020.1745629.

11. Milton Friedman, *Capitalism and Freedom* (Chicago: University of Chicago Press, 1962), 166, cited in Longoria, "Meritocracy and Americans' Views on Distributive Justice," 23.

12. John Rawls, *A Theory of Justice* (Cambridge: Harvard University Press, 1971), 64.

13. Longoria, "Meritocracy and Americans' Views on Distributive Justice," 22.

14. Longoria, "Meritocracy and Americans' Views on Distributive Justice," 18.

15. John Gardner, *Excellence: Can We Be Equal and Excellent Too?* (New York: Harper Bros., 1961), 67, cited in Joseph F. Kett, *Merit: The History of a Founding Ideal from the American Revolution to the Twenty-First Century* (Ithaca, NY: Cornell University Press, 2012), 228.

16. Angela L. Duckworth, Christopher Peterson, Michael D. Matthews, and Dennis R. Kelly, "Grit: Perseverance and Passion for Long-Term Goals," *Journal of Personality and Social Psychology* 92, no. 6 (2007): 1087–88.

17. Emmie Martin, "How One 31-Year-Old Paid Off $220,000 in Student Loans in 3 Years," *Business Insider*, March 8, 2017, https://www.businessinsider.com/how-ebony-horton-paid-off-220000-worth-of-student-loans-in-3-years-2017-3.

18. Gretchen Lancour (@gretchenlancour), Twitter post, March 10, 2017, cited in Amanda Fama, "Internet Drags Girl for Unrelatable Student Loan Hack," *Elite Daily*, March 10, 2017, https://www.elitedaily.com/social-news/girl-unrelatable-hack-pay-220k-loan/1821259.

19. Robert L. Simon, "Equality, Merit, and the Determination of Our Gifts," *Social Research* 41, no. 3 (1974): 497.

4. Merit without the *-ocracy*

1. Patricia Lewis, Ruth Simpson, and Ruth Sealy, "Changing Perceptions of Meritocracy in Senior Women's Careers," *Gender in Management: An International Journal* 25, no. 3 (2010): 184–97.

2. James R. Kluegel and Eliot R. Smith, *Beliefs about Inequality: Americans' Views of What Is and What Ought to Be* (Chicago: Aldine, 1986).

3. Sherry B. Ortner, *New Jersey Dreaming: Capital, Culture, and the Class of '58* (Durham: Duke University Press, 2003), 5.

4. Christopher Hayes, *Twilight of the Elites: America after Meritocracy* (New York: Broadway Books, 2013).

5. Robert K. Miller and Stephen J. McNamee, *The Meritocracy Myth* (Lanham, MD: Rowman & Littlefield, 2013), 2.

5. What's Deserve Got to Do with It?

1. Helaine Olen, "Ivanka Trump Comes Out against All Guaranteed Jobs Except Her Own," *Washington Post*, February 26, 2019, https://www.washingtonpost.com/opinions/2019/02/26/ivanka-trump-comes-out-against-all-guaranteed-jobs-except-her-own/.

2. Kenneth Vogel (@kenvogel), Twitter post, February 26, 2019, https://twitter.com/kenvogel/status/1100430221503811586?lang=en.

3. Eugene Scott (@Eugene_Scott), Twitter post, February 26, 2019, https://twitter.com/eugene_scott/status/1100404155619991552.

4. Sarah Jones, "Ivanka Trump, Famous Nepotism Hire, Says People Want to Work for What They Get," *New York Magazine*, February 26, 2019, https://nymag.com/intelligencer/2019/02/ivanka-trump-nepotism-hire-people-dont-want-handouts.html.

5. The Daily Show (@TheDailyShow), Twitter post, February 26, 2019, https://twitter.com/thedailyshow/status/1100430474462269441?lang=en.

6. Ivanka Trump, *The Trump Card: Playing to Win in Work and Life* (New York: Simon and Schuster, 2009), 1–2.

7. Jo Littler, *Against Meritocracy* (New York: Routledge, 2017).

8. Paul Ryan (@SpeakerRyan), Twitter post, September 2, 2017, https://twit ter.com/SpeakerRyan/status/904008582290710528.

9. Brandon Friedman (@BFriedmanDC), Twitter post, September 2, 2017, https://twitter.com/BFriedmanDC/status/904210351952207872.

10. Daniel Markovits, *The Meritocracy Trap: How America's Foundational Myth Feeds Inequality, Dismantles the Middle Class, and Devours the Elite* (New York: Penguin, 2019), 273.

11. Markovits, *The Meritocracy Trap*, xiii, xi, xxi.

12. Christopher Hayes, *Twilight of the Elites: America after Meritocracy* (New York: Broadway Books, 2013), 57.

13. Thomas Mulligan, *Justice and the Meritocratic State* (New York: Routledge, 2017).

14. Sarah F. Brosnan and Frans B. M. De Waal, "Monkeys Reject Unequal Pay," *Nature* 425, no. 6955 (2003): 297–99.

15. Jill Filipovic, "When Honest Women Replace 'Self-Made' Men," *New York Times*, January 11, 2019, https://www.nytimes.com/2019/01/11/opinion/sunday/pelosi-congress-women.html.

16. Dena M. Bravata et al., "Prevalence, Predictors, and Treatment of Impostor Syndrome: A Systematic Review," *Journal of General Internal Medicine* (2019): 1–24.

17. David Williams and Gianluca Mezzofiore, "Penn State Football Player Receives Letter Criticizing His Dreadlocks," CNN, October 9, 2019, https://www.cnn.com/2019/10/08/us/penn-state-player-letter-trnd/index.html.

18. Richard Sennett and Jonathan Cobb, *The Hidden Injuries of Class* (New York: Alfred A. Knopf, 1972).

19. Melvin J. Lerner and Dale T. Miller, "Just World Research and the Attribution Process: Looking Back and Ahead," *Psychological Bulletin* 85, no. 5 (1978): 1030.

20. Mark Jacobson, "Bernie Sanders for President? You Frickin' Kidding Me? He's a Commie. Is That Even Legal, a Communist President?" *New York Magazine*, December 28, 2014, http://nymag.com/daily/intelligencer/2014/12/bernie-sanders-for-president-why-not.html.

21. Trump, *The Trump Card*, 6.

22. Jhumpa Bhattacharya and Anne Price, "The Power of Narrative in Economic Development," Economic Security Project, November 8, 2019, https://medium.com/economicsecproj/the-power-of-narrative-in-economic-policy-27bd8a9ed888.

Index

Book titles are indexed under the author's name. Newspapers, journals, films, and TV shows are listed alphabetically by title. Individuals interviewed appear under the entry, "interviews and interviewees."